Encounters: Experience and Anthropological Knowledge

ISSN: 1746-8175

Series Editor: John Borneman

The Encounters: Experience and Anthropological Knowledge series examines the issues that affect all anthropologists in the field. These short collections of essays describe and analyze the surprise and interest of the fieldwork encounter, on topics such as money, violence and love. The series aims to show that anthropological knowledge is based in experience, bringing into the public realm useful and thought-provoking areas for discussion that previously anthropologists have been reluctant or unable to highlight.

Money
Ethnographic Encounters

Edited by

STEFAN SENDERS AND ALLISON TRUITT

Oxford • New York

English edition
First published in 2007 by
Berg
Editorial offices:
First Floor, Angel Court, 81 St Clements Street, Oxford OX4 1AW, UK
175 Fifth Avenue, New York, NY 10010, USA

Berg is the imprint of Oxford International Publishers Ltd.

Library of Congress Cataloging-in-Publication Data
Money : ethnographic encounters / edited by Stefan Senders and Allison
Truitt. — English ed.
   p. cm.
Includes bibliographical references and index.
Papers first presented at the 2004 meeting of the American
Ethnological Society in Atlanta, Georgia, in a session on "Encounters
with Money."
   ISBN-13: 978-1-84520-750-2 (cloth)
   ISBN-10: 1-84520-750-5 (cloth)
   ISBN-13: 978-1-84520-751-9 (pbk.)
   ISBN-10: 1-84520-751-3 (pbk.)
   1. Anthropology—Field work—Finance—Congresses. 2.
Anthropology—Research—Finance—Congresses. 3. Anthropology—
Research grants—Congresses. I. Senders, Stefan John, 1959- II. Truitt,
Allison. III. American Ethnological Society. Meeting (2004 : Atlanta,
Ga.)

   GN34.3.F53M66 2007
   306.4—dc22   2007023995

British Library Cataloguing-in-Publication Data
A catalogue record for this book is available from the British Library.

ISBN 978 1 84520 750 2 (Cloth)
        978 1 84520 751 9 (Paper)

Typeset by Avocet Typeset, Chilton, Aylesbury, Bucks
Printed in the United Kingdom by Biddles Ltd, King's Lynn

www.bergpublishers.com

Contents

Acknowledgments

This volume began as a series of papers first presented at the 2004 meeting of the American Ethnological Society in Atlanta, Georgia, in a session on "Encounters with Money." We would like to express thanks to John Borneman who first proposed the series and asked us to participate, and who was always willing to help. We would like to thank the following people for their assistance in putting this volume together: Bryan Lentz, Tonia Saxon, Hannah Shakespeare, and two anonymous reviewers. Any project of this sort requires the work and goodwill of numerous people, some highly visible – reviewers, editors, writers – and some less so – friends, partners, students. We can't hope to thank individually everyone who has helped us, but we offer our thanks nonetheless. We are particularly grateful to the authors for working so hard to meet the many deadlines along the way, and for their understanding when hurricanes – both atmospheric and institutional – prevented us from meeting our own deadlines.

Notes on Contributors

John Borneman is Professor of Anthropology at Princeton University. His initial fieldwork was in Germany, and he has been working most recently in Lebanon and Syria. He has written widely on political and legal anthropology, kinship, European integration, and the socialism and post-socialist transformations of East-Central Europe. His most recent book is *Syrian Episodes: Sons, Fathers, and an Anthropologist in Aleppo*.

Julie Y. Chu is a sociocultural anthropologist whose book, *Cosmologies of Credit: Fuzhounese Migration and the Politics of Destination* (Duke University: forthcoming), examines transnational mobility and value transformation in post-Mao China. She is currently Assistant Professor of Anthropology at Wellesley College. Her broader interests include material and visual culture, ritual life, state governmentality and the mediation of social space and historical consciousness.

J.A. Dickinson is Assistant Professor of Anthropology at the University of Vermont. Her research combines linguistic anthropology and economic anthropology of post-socialism, with a focus on rural Ukraine. Her most recent project focuses on advertising, consumer culture and language in contemporary Ukraine.

Naeem Inayatullah is Associate Professor of Politics at Ithaca College. His main fields are international relations theory and the history of political economy. He is co-author (with David Blaney) of *International Relations and the Problem of Difference* (Routledge 2004), and co-editor (with Robin Riley) of *Interrogating Imperialism: Conversations on Gender, Race, and War* (Palgrave 2006). He is working on a manuscript titled *Savage Economy: Wealth, Poverty, and Capitalism's Necro-Economics*.

Ellen Moodie, Assistant Professor of Anthropology at the University of Illinois at Urbana-Champaign, is working on the manuscript "'It's Worse than the War': Crime, Talk and Transition in El Salvador's Postwar Era." Based on fieldwork begun shortly after the 1992 peace accords, it examines fragments of postwar experience entextualized in discourses of security and insecurity.

Marty Otañez is a postdoctoral fellow in the Tobacco Control Research Center, University of California, San Francisco. His research focuses on labor, globalization, and public health. Otañez co-produced three documentary films, *Thangata* and *Up in Smoke* about tobacco workers in Malawi, and *120,000 Lives* on smoking in Hollywood movies.

Stefan Senders is Assistant Professor of Writing and Rhetoric at Hobart and William Smith Colleges in Geneva, N.Y. He holds a Ph.D. in Anthropology from Cornell University, and has conducted research in Berlin, Germany; Ghana, West Africa; and Toast, North Carolina. He is currently working on an epistemology of risk, and on historical research into legibility and illegibility in medicine.

Allison Truitt is Assistant Professor of Anthropology at Tulane University in New Orleans, Louisiana. Her research interests focus on the interplay between economic forms and cultural practices in Vietnam. She has published on the cultural politics of currency reforms in *Research in Economic Anthropology*.

Preface

John Borneman

Money: Ethnographic Encounters is a collection of essays about fieldwork experiences of contemporary anthropologists. Its focus, like that of other volumes to follow in this series, is on personal encounters that betray an intimacy with difference but that tend to be omitted from standard academic accounts. In this volume the authors explore the role of money in the anthropological encounter.

Modern Anthropology is different from the other human sciences because it takes the intimate experiences of fieldwork to be a primary source of knowledge. Anthropological and ethnographic knowledge is most often produced through "fieldwork," a form of long-term experiential study that brings the researcher into direct contact with an "Other." Anthropologists have, of course, incorporated methods and techniques of other disciplines – history (archival work), literature (reading texts), linguistics (discourse transcriptions) and psychology (controlled experimentation); and scholars in a wide range of disciplines have made use of ethnographic techniques. But while ethnography has become an important tool in many disciplines, its success has come with more than a few vexing questions. Is *any* place a field site? Should reading in the archives be regarded as an encounter with an Other who speaks back to the researcher through the text? Are all field sites equally valuable or productive?

Such questions challenge anthropologists' assumptions about their unique contributions to the understanding of culture and about the relative value of the risks they take in ethnographic encounters. To the extent that anthropologists have succumbed to a professionalization and standardization in style of presentation, their accounts are often dismissed as obsessed with the everyday or, alternately, as overly ambitious theoretical renderings of simple things. The specific cultural texture of person and place is all too frequently sacrificed for a more streamlined theoretical account that focuses solely on a particular question or problem. Moreover, since the disappearance of "the primitive" as an object of study, the public tends to be confused about what it is, exactly, that ethnographers do.

In this first volume, edited and with a theoretical introduction by Stefan Senders and Allison Truitt, encounters with money are drawn from ethnographic fieldwork in Malawi, China, Vietnam, El Salvador, Germany, Ukraine and Pakistan. These accounts reveal some of the ways that money is, as Senders and Truitt write, "an indispensable, and in some cases, even compulsory mode of communication in fieldwork." Not only does every anthropologist have a different history of money that they are asked to share in the field, but also their access to others is dependent on having (and often giving) money. Once financing for fieldwork is obtained, most anthropologists still find themselves on relatively tight budgets. But while poor at home, most anthropologists find themselves well-off compared to the relatively poor people they most often meet in the field. These inequalities ultimately structure many research choices, such as types of informants or sites, and they shape some of the ethical values that anthropologists embrace, such as the defense of marginality and resistance to authority.

The authors here tell stories of intimate encounters – reflexive, doubting, partial, immediate – that somehow "jar the anthropologist's subjective sense of social relations and social order." Against the prevailing view of the universality of money, they demonstrate that its meaning is variable and contingent, dependent on very particular relations that always seem to make them complicitous in the experience of their informants. Money, they show, creates value (including the value of the anthropologist), yields to or resists processes of commodification, works as a source of redemption, assuages guilt or creates access, or becomes a creative force of personal identification.

We asked the authors to write with a particular concern in mind: to focus on stories that showed their own engagement with money in fieldwork, and that demonstrated money's importance in learning about cultural difference. We also requested that they resist the temptation to let theoretical concerns dominate their writing. We encouraged them instead to allow their descriptions of fieldwork to show how and in what way cultural difference is learned in an encounter with money. We invited them, in other words, to write outside the current normative genres of anthropology, and of the academy generally, and to risk exposing themselves – warts, private pleasures, misunderstandings and all – in the thick of it. Hence contributors have elaborated their specific interactions and eschewed most of the conventions that authorize ethnographic accounts, such as footnoting, long bibliographies or dense theoretical language.

Such rhetorical change makes new demands on our readers: we ask them to enter, openly, into the often threatening, sometimes embarrassing, but always potentially insight-bearing situations of fieldwork. In return, we hope that the reading of these essays awakens an appreciation for the subjective and interdisciplinary quality of sensual experience (personal, tied to a particular time and place); for curiosity in difference itself, in translating the strange, foreign or unassimilable; and for a kind of storytelling that contributes both to the documentary function of the ethnographic encounter and to its analytical potential.

Introduction

Stefan Senders and Allison Truitt

In *Money: Ethnographic Encounters*, anthropologists offer first-hand accounts of fieldwork, paying particular attention to experiences they call "encounters" with money. Their stories, from a range of field sites including Malawi, China, Vietnam, El Salvador, Germany, Ukraine and Pakistan, are more descriptive than theoretical, more narrative that analytical. They reveal some of the ways money both expands and limits the relationships that make anthropology unique and productive. They demonstrate, moreover, the specific kind of insights that only experiential accounts can generate.

We want to be clear from the outset that our project here is not to produce an "anthropology of money." Many such books have been written, and many of them are wonderful sources of insight into money as a cultural and trans-cultural object. We recognize the value of such works, and we have learned a great deal from them. Some, such as Simmel's *The Philosophy of Money* (1990 [1907]), Bloch and Parry's *Money and the Morality of Exchange* (1989) and Hart's *Money in an Unequal World* (2001), we have found particularly valuable. But our project here is somewhat different. We take money as our starting point, and we inquire into ways and occasions when it moves us into ethnographic experiences that seem particularly productive. We are interested in the ways anthropologists produce knowledge, and particularly in the ways anthropologists produce knowledge from their ethnographic fieldwork. The book, in other words, is about knowledge, and it examines experiences with money as a way of observing processes of knowledge-production.

Anthropologists have, by and large, ignored the role of money in their research. As anthropologists become familiar with their field sites, they tend to forget, at least in their official capacity as anthropologists, about the role that money plays in their work; money quickly fades into the texture of everyday life, eluding examination. Money is quietly buried in stories about other things – travel, funding, access – and the ways money serves in the field as a site of cultural investment is overlooked.

In the field, money is an indispensable and often compulsory mode of communication. Perhaps more than any other object, force or sign, money gives initial shape to fieldwork relationships; even before the work begins, anthropologists fantasize, speculate and budget for a future about which they know little. Their concepts and approaches are shaped by the orientations of granting agencies. They try to calculate how long they will be able to stay, how much they will be able to spend and how much their cash will be worth, whether in terms of material or labor. Once in the field, they must learn what counts as currency, and how currency counts, in their new environment, and they are forced by necessity to become aware of the locally appropriate ways money circulates and functions.

Money, because it is so often seen as a "universal" commodity, a medium of exchange that honors no local particularity, is often the source, or site, of the experiences we call "encounter." We focus on the "encounter" as a defining act in the production of anthropological knowledge. With that focus we begin to see the autonomy of the anthropologist yield to mutual participation; the voice of ethnographic authority gives way to an ironic mode as moments of crisis, of failure and of misunderstanding come to be central themes in our stories. The "encounter" thus brings differences into greater relief, heightening and articulating them, while at the same time affirming that even radical difference is no obstacle to understanding.

Anthropology's claim to disciplinary uniqueness and value still largely rests, despite several decades of critiques, on its method – participant-observation. As anthropologists, we *know* because we *engage*, we *participate*, we *observe*. But what is it, specifically, about participation that is so powerful? The best anthropological work, as well as some of the most controversial scandals in the discipline, is rooted in the special intimacy of fieldwork. By developing intimacy and familiarity with others in the context of long-term fieldwork, anthropologists claim to produce authentic knowledge about culture. It is not enough to stay in the field for months or years, or to be fluent in the language of the field; the anthropologist is expected to cross, even if only for brief periods, from the position of observing *knower* to that of intimate *participant*. While such work may require long periods in the field, anthropological insights tend to come suddenly, as the products of "encounter." The moments of "encounter" are assumed to arise, unbidden, from our own participation in the lives of others.

While intimacy and patience are critical to the production of anthropological knowledge, not all interactions are equally likely to produce encounters. When we asked the authors included in this collection to write about encounters with money, they all, without our prompting, produced narratives with a shared theme: they described moments when their security – whether granted by superior knowledge, state support or material advantage – failed them. They described events that showed their weaknesses, their vulnerability. What is significant about a cultural encounter, as we use the term, then, is that it jars the anthropologist's subjective sense of social relations and social order, and even more specifically, it brings the anthropologist and her "subject" into a world of shared risk. No longer protected by aura, state authority or material armor, the anthropologist experiences a shared sense of moral vertigo and disability. This breach constitutes the foundation for what philosopher Charles Taylor called a "language of perspicuous contrast," a language in which all cultural experience might be seen clearly in relation to a third or shared position. Only when the anthropologist is no longer emboldened by the authorities of technology, violence, power and mobility – all of which can find their expression in the form of money – may she experience encounter. In this way, the encounter not only confirms the density and singularity of ethnographic experience, but it also reveals the complicity of the anthropologist in the very act by which difference is made manifest and conscious. The encounter, then, sheds light on the production of culture through the experience of difference. Or, to put it another way, the encounter demonstrates that culture needs to be, at least in part, understood as an epistemological process, rather than an ontological object; it is something we create from knowing, not what we know merely by seeing or experiencing. Our task in this volume is to illuminate the nature of these experiences by letting insights from cultural encounters – reflexive, doubting, partial and immediate – stand on their own.

While we stress the importance of immediacy and sensory ruptures, to the extent that the anthropologists in this volume represent their experiences textually, their elaboration of encounter is retrospective. Meaning arises in the rhetorical elaboration of the encounter, and in the reflection that follows the anthropologist's initial confusion, embarrassment and anxiety. These essays consequently place value on the storytelling rather than analysis removed from location and buffered by theory. The authors have rejected typical conventions that authorize ethnographic accounts, such as footnoting, long bibliographies or dense theoretical language. Instead they offer highly descriptive narrative accounts that are more concerned with the texture of person and place than with marshaling evidence for a particular theory. In this sense the authors relinquish theory, the meta-language that produces the translatability of encounters, and that converts anthropological experience into professional and academic capital.

Given that the authors have left their capital behind, perhaps it is no coincidence that all the essays share rhetorical strategies in which the anthropologist plays the fool or the dupe. The ironic effect conveys the uncertainty that characterizes fieldwork and so highlights what we have come to regard as a precondition for anthropological knowledge. We see these essays as part of ongoing conversations about knowledge, power and money; we see them as a start, not the last word. (For readers interested in following or joining the conversation, we have provided an annotated reading guide.)

Money and Anthropological Encounter

What is the source of purchasing power in China? How should one dispose of unspent rupees at the Islamabad airport? Why do some people insist that the Ukrainian currency was printed with a grammatical error? How can a stranger's request for money in Santa Tecla, El Salvador, seem so extraordinary yet so believable? In this volume we address these questions in light of larger overarching questions: How do anthropologists experience money in the field? What do those experiences teach us about culture? What does the anthropologist's relation to money suggest about anthropological knowledge and the ways we produce it?

Our claim that money generally escapes ethnographic scrutiny is not to suggest that anthropologists have ignored money. Anthropological studies have demonstrated repeatedly that even as money is imagined as global in scope, the meanings that accrue to money are historically and socially situated. More telling, though, is that most anthropologists have ignored the ways money intrudes on and shapes their own inquiries. We very rarely hear of the anthropologist's money, of the cost of work, of the price of currency. The inconvenient fact that fieldwork experience may require outside financing, and that such financing shapes the questions anthropologists ask, is not so much hidden as marginalized, a necessary yet peripheral concern. Yet money enables anthropologists to purchase the mobility and means to carry out field research. Without money in hand, anthropologists would have no means of collapsing the distance between themselves and others, and it is money that allows them to constitute their object of study by transforming distance into difference.

Anthropologists have historically identified their object – the primitive – in a rhetorical juxtaposition with modernity (Fabian 1983). The rhetorical strategy entails a dislocation in both time and space, a chronotope of cultural difference that has been, not surprisingly, expressed and experienced in terms of money. Money has in fact served as a compressed metaphor for temporal relationships. Money has often indexed the distinction between "monetary" and "pre-monetary" systems of exchange; its *presence* has signified the difference between historically "modern" and "not-yet-modern" states or cultures. Anthropologists, by virtue of their relation to money, have distinguished and constituted their objects as *behind them in time* (historically glossed as "the primitive"), a temporal lag exemplified by forms of "non-economic" and specifically "non-monetary" exchange. An exemplary illustration is Mary Douglas' (1958) analysis of the distribution of raffia among the Lele in Central Africa. She describes the Lele as "on the verge of a market economy" (1958: 109), and midway through her analysis, she admits frustration at not being able to purchase everyday objects for her ethnographic collection:

> I had great difficulty trying to buy ordinary domestic objects with francs. They had no traditional price, as they usually changed hands on kinship lines, with an "acknowledgement fee" of one or two cloths. My friends, mistaking this fee for a price equivalent for the value of the goods, tried to persuade reluctant sellers that they ought to part with their things for 10 or 20 francs, the official equivalent of one or two raffia cloths. However, even if I doubled the number of francs, they were still not willing to sell. For raffia cloth they would have sold willingly, but my ethnographic collection seemed doomed, since I could not buy raffia cloth. (1958: 115)

By the end of the essay, Douglas transforms her failure to purchase everyday objects into anthropological capital. Raffia cloth has not developed into a form of primitive money, she concludes, because most goods are distributed without buying and selling, thus resolving the categorical status of state-issue currency and raffia cloth. Douglas ends her impasse, one both theoretical and pragmatic, not with encounter, but with a payment of tribute to the discipline of economics, a brief nod to the economist Karl Menger.

In other ethnographic cases, "intimacy" is premised on the absence of money. In contrast to Douglas' disappointment with money's failure to sate her acquisitive desire, E.E. Evans-Pritchard describes his initial purchases as trivial: "[I] proceeded to Nuerland ... with my tent, some equipment, and a few stores bought at Malakal, and two servants, an Atwot and a Bellanda, picked up hastily at the same place" (1940: 9). Once in Nuerland, however, he only gains acceptance after acquiring cattle, the very idiom of sociality (13). What, though, did Evans-Pritchard sacrifice in order to acquire those cattle? We are not told, but we do know that among the Nuer, one cannot acquire surplus. Evans-Pritchard admits that "the only way of keeping tobacco among the Nuer is to deny that one possesses it and to keep it well-hidden" (184), an image that foreshadows accumulation's dependency on secrecy and concealment. No anthropologist working today would be surprised to find money in the field, but the historical bias remains.

We raise several questions regarding anthropological perspectives on money. How do ethnographers cultivate intimacy in the face of commodity relations? That anthropologists often overlook their own position with regard to money is due, in part, to the field's demand for "intimacy" and therefore frequently depends on the denial of commoditization. In a sense, the intimacy of ethnographic fieldwork reenacts the separation of the public and private spheres described by Habermas (1991). In Europe, the intimacy of the private sphere, "the domain of pure humanity," depended on its being considered isolated from commodity relations (46). It was this conceptual emancipation that allowed the bourgeois family to imagine itself as intimate yet autonomous. Ethnography reproduces the same dichotomy in its frequent refusal to examine or engage money.

The introduction of money into fieldwork relationships appears to entail the commoditization of culture itself, and it risks exposing the intimacy cultivated in fieldwork as nothing more than commodity exchange. Money in the field can thus appear to "debase" culture itself. Money is often seen as supplemental to culture, functioning beneath, behind or in addition to it.

Another question concerns the tension between money as cultural material and money as a representation of abstract value that arises out of circulation. Anthropologists tend to locate money within local systems, a perspective well articulated by Parry and Bloch (1989), who claim that anthropologists should not assume that money gives rise to a worldview, rather they should attend to "the existing worldview[s] [that] give rise to particular ways of representing money" (19). Anthropologists have also demonstrated that money is a material *of* and *for* cultural difference and transformation. In studies of post-socialist and post-colonial regimes, money has emerged as a key symbol of state-led economic polices, as an index of transformations in the value of labor-power, and as a barometer of economic instability (see Robbins and Akin 1999, Lemon 1998, Verdery 1996, Guyer 1994a). In these studies, money is again compressed, not as a metaphor for temporal relationships but for *stable* and *unstable* states, *legitimate* and *illegitimate* regimes, and political conditions of *normality* and *crisis*.

Historically, anthropologists have had more power than the people they study, and to a large extent this differential holds true today. That power has generally been reflective of international relations, such as colonialism, the Cold War or global economic trends, and it has been most profoundly and immediately expressed by money. Anthropological fieldwork, then, is most often conducted under circumstances of economic inequality; anthropologists, when they have more money and material wealth than the people they study, are sought out for their wealth or access to power, and anthropologists use that pecuniary attraction to their own advantage. As anthropologists have come to recognize the ways such inequality shapes their work, there have been increasing calls for projects that "anthropologize the West" (Rabinow 1986: 241) and "study up" (Nader 1974).

Anthropologists have responded to these calls by turning to new ethnographic objects, such as the role played by technology in shaping the interpretative practices of price (Zaloom 2003) and the forms of reasoning employed by technocratic (Riles 2004) and financial experts (Ho 2005). While such research addresses some of the relevant economic and power imbalances that have characterized fieldwork, it still leaves open the question of how money shapes ethnographic experience and anthropological knowledge. Whether one studies "up, down, or sideways," to paraphrase Laura Nader, money remains a potent site of investment. Yet for the reasons we have outlined above – the desire for intimacy, the emphasis on the local, and the appeal of finance – ethnographers often exclude from their purview the important ways money shapes ethnographic experience.

In this volume, we give priority to money in its intimate form, and all our discussion of money in the abstract is built on that foundation. Each contributor details an encounter with money in its most concrete and generative yet anonymous form – cash. As the essays demonstrate, money, while often theorized as an abstraction, is made more fully comprehensible with reference to our experiences handling it. Moreover, the symbolic value of currency – of particular coins and bills – generates fantasies of greater, not smaller, scales of exchange. Cash circulates as a material trace of fantasies of nationhood and global markets. Moreover, the value of anthropologists is often enhanced when they are identified with the near-universal idiom of the global marketplace – the U.S. dollar. It would be a mistake to assume that the dollar is prevalent in the stories presented here just because the contributors are based at higher-education institutions in the United States; rather, the focus on the U.S. dollar reflects empirical findings – the dollar assumes the role of a universal translator of value, a compressed sign of the inequitable relations that configure current social orders. The fact that cash conjures up such fantasies poses a challenge to what appear to be "face-to-face" interactions. These essays demonstrate in different ways that the value or meaning of the encounter cannot be determined at the moment of exchange. Like money, encounter is a placeholder for an imaginary meeting point between subjects.

Despite the certainty of power, the position of the anthropologist as the *knower* cannot be secured through monetary transactions. Money allows proximity, even as it establishes distance between the anthropologist and his or her subjects, distance that is simultaneously dissolved and maintained through monetary exchanges. At the same time, the uncertainty that permeates these encounters is marked by discrepancies in economic power. While fieldwork is conventionally held to be based on intimacy and experience – e.g. participating and observing – anthropologists also participate in networks that are not fully visible to their subjects. Anthropologists often rely on funding or sources of money that arrive from other locations in the form of grants, savings or loans. Although anthropologists place value on mutual participation, they draw on money from outside the visible economy, hence the "value" of anthropologist's work is both prior (e.g. recognition granted by funding agencies) and belated (represented by the translation of fieldwork into ethnographic writing) to the encounter.

We have collected stories of ethnographic encounters, and of the role money plays in them, to illuminate the complex relationship between money and anthropological experience and knowledge. It is a shifting relationship, and one that we expect will require more study. We now introduce the essays in this volume, the first in a series of books examining the ethnographic encounter.

Economic Reforms and Credibility

In this volume the authors exchange stories and cash, and as they do, questions of credibility, reliability and faith – moral questions – come to the fore. The first two essays focus on the reliability of currency and goods in China and Ukraine, two countries that have recently undergone significant social and economic reforms. In both cases, the anthropologist requires a guide to the rapidly changing conditions of the marketplace. In "Equation Fixations: On the Whole and the Sum of Dollars in Foreign

Exchange," Julie Chu struggles to understand and negotiate cultural values entailed in the exchange of goods and cash. Chu draws the reader into the anticipated pleasure of shopping in China. There, she imagined, she would enjoy wealth derived from the superior value of the U.S. dollar, at that time exchanged for the Chinese *reminbi* (RMB) at a rate of 8:1. Spending, as Georg Simmel (1950) theorized, could be described as the sudden climax and dissipation of potential associated with the marketplace. The pleasure of fieldwork becomes mingled with the erotics of shopping as Chu describes how her accidental glance rouses a street vendor: "to linger over an object, as I did with this T-shirt, was to invest it with consumer desire and potential market value." But the climax and dissipation of inquiry is characterized by ambivalence and transference. Spending and consumption, as seen in this essay, take the form of displaced eroticism and thus provide seemingly *safe* forms of erotic interaction (important in these days of AIDS). Chu, however, finds that nothing in the Chinese marketplace is "transparent or secure" – neither the goods nor the money used as payment. She must learn the art of "solicit price, return price" from Liyan, a wily Chinese shopper. Still she confesses the shopping in China was a constant source of embarrassment and stress. These encounters prompt her to revisit her initial thought that it was the magical exchange rate of 8:1 that led people to fixate on the U.S. dollar as both "better" and "bigger."

In "Changing Money in Post-Soviet Ukraine," J.A. Dickinson investigates the expressive power of cash itself; specifically, she shows how the Ukraine's newly redesigned and minted currency serves as a diagnostic tool for citizens' appraisal of their government's legitimacy. While for Chu shopping was a focus of desire and a constant source of embarrassment, Dickinson describes the marketplace as a realm of danger. The privileged position her dollars enjoyed was not based on their circulation external to the marketplace; rather, the U.S. dollar was powerful because it had maintained its value in the face of the demise of the Soviet Union. In her essay, Dickinson examines how currency stands as a proxy for state power and authority, a relationship that introduces "the state" and the realm of "the international" into the intimacy of fieldwork. Dickinson is confronted by the new meanings associated with the market following the collapse of the Soviet Union. The market is now a place of danger, exemplified above all by the illegal currency traders who appear to control the flow of cash. Unlike the illegal currency traders she meets, Dickinson is an emissary of legal money, both U.S. dollars and the new Ukrainian national currency. When she brings the newly issued notes to her host family, they criticize the bills, suggesting that they were designed and produced care-lessly and incompetently. Their observations compel her to examine how people evaluate and react to the newly issued national currency, and how those responses reflect their unease with the Ukrainian national move-ment. Dickenson's account also suggests that her most important insights emerged from her most embarrassing failures. She learns about local value when she accidentally reveals her ignorance of the cultural value of the U.S. dollar, and when she finds herself corrected or ignored.

The U.S. dollar figures in both essays as a currency of a parallel economy, but in surprisingly different circuits of exchange. In China, the U.S. dollar signifies wealth that is both bigger and better than what can be domestically produced. In the Ukrainian borderlands, the inventory of U.S. dollars is in the hands of the currency traders, signaling the triumph of the market over the legitimacy of the Ukrainian nation. As the next two essays demonstrate, the U.S. dollar also intrudes into personal relations in the field, reducing intimacy and confidence to the alienated relations of the marketplace.

Suffering and Redemption

Anthropologists are often embarrassed by the place of money in their own research. Fieldwork, so dependent on intimate encounters and relation-ships, is particularly sensitive to potential devaluation through commodi-tization. In the next two essays, Ellen Moodie and Allison Truitt find themselves identified with the U.S. dollar, a symbol of the enormous flow of wealth from the United States to post-war El Salvador and Vietnam; their experiences and stories demonstrate in intimate terms the ways money mediates the expression of good faith in personal relations. The stories they tell suggest an uneasy equation of suffering, redemption and money; in both cases a "story" of suffering is exchanged for money. How, they ask, should the anthropologist confront the problems of credibility and reliability that lie at the heart of the anthropologist's epistemological dilemma? In the end, the question is not whether the stories are "counter-feit" or not, but how they function as cultural currency.

In "Dollars and *Dolores* in Postwar El Salvador," Ellen Moodie offers money as a token of her desire to enter into exchanges. Can money, she asks, convert suffering into redemption? Moodie reflects on a begging stranger's claim to be a Quaker and a near-stranger's claim to have ovarian cancer; how should she regard such stories? Do they merely represent the assumption that she, as a *gringa*, will be gullible? She rationalizes her responses in a series of calculative associations: the cost of a cup of cap-puccino, her mother's death, the obligations of a sister-in-law. At issue is not only her position as "the *gringa*," but also the question of faith – should she believe the stories of suffering? Ultimately, her encounters reflect on anthropological fieldwork: How does one enter into meaningful exchange-relations with others in the field? She recognizes the epistemological and ethical crisis; yet, her association with money forces her to consider herself as misrepresented and misrepresenting without resolution. The ongoing exchange – of stories, of belief and doubt, of money – erodes her sense of authority, and finally leaves her open to new forms of knowledge.

In a story of another city haunted by its own violent past, Allison Truitt tells of her relationship with Mr. Thang, an impoverished amputee war veteran and failing entrepreneur living in Saigon, Vietnam. In "Hot Loans and Cold Cash in Saigon," Thang and Truitt are "friends" and they have helped each other in a variety of ways – with money, time and sympathy. Thang routinely attempts to borrow money from Truitt by telling sob-stories, which Truitt resists. Eventually Truitt discovers that Thang has acquired a large loan based on the claim that Truitt would be sending him money and giving him a motorbike; moreover, she discovers, she will be expected to confirm his claim, and thus become responsible for the debt; Truitt has become collateral. When Truitt realizes she has been converted into symbolic and financial capital, and that the intimacy of their relation-ship has been put on the market, she is forced to examine her own role as a foreigner in the Vietnamese social economy. In the heat of the sudden economic ruptures associated with Vietnam's integration into the global economy, she finds encounter comes not so much because of her associ-ation with money, but because, through a combination of sympathetic magic (Frazer 1922) and sacrifice (Bloch and Parry 1982), she has been symbolically transformed *into* money.

In El Salvador and Vietnam, the U.S. dollar is often portrayed as a potent symbol of wealth and redemption. The massive return remittances from family members now residing in the United States have provided an infusion of cash that threatens to overturn the traditional distinctions of kin- and market-based exchanges. The anthropologists in this volume do not focus on those long-distance transactions in which money's value is wired instantaneously across national borders; instead they examine encounters that are at once more intimate and estranging. Moodie and Truitt struggle with their own subjective understandings of these intimate economies. By contrast, Marty Otañez and Stefan Senders confront with embarrassment and shame the source of their symbolic value.

The Source of Power

The essays by Otañez and Senders demonstrate some of the ways anthropologists use money, whether as "gift" or "payment," to establish connections, assuage guilt and gain access. In "The Smoking Wallet: An Anthropologist Meets Transnational Tobacco Corporations in Malawi," Otañez confronts the uncomfortable realization that his most valued research contact, Eugene, a local trade union activist, also works with and accepts gifts from Philip Morris, a transnational tobacco corporation. Although the gifts Otañez offers are far smaller than those offered by the corporation, both Otañez and Philip Morris use the same strategy to legitimize their projects. Otañez asks himself whether he can think of himself as an exception to the local dynamic of dependency, characterized by impersonal and infrequent exchanges between Westerners and locals in Malawi. The moment is excruciating; Otañez is invested in his work, both morally and financially, and his faith in his own moral goodness is challenged by his discovery that he is not appreciably different from the corporation he fights. The crisis leads to a renewed commitment; Otañez concludes that he must become more active in struggling against corporations of which he disapproves, and that his academic work must in some way change to fit into that project. The encounter in the essay is defined not by the particularities of an experience or relationship, but by changes internal to the anthropologist, changes in his own values; to put it another way, he may have cash – but can he make change?

In contrast, Stefan Senders queries how his fieldwork experiences in Europe and Africa were shaped by his association with money. While in Ghana in the 1980s, Senders finds that he holds the ultimate fetish – money. Because he comes from the United States and because he holds American currency, women want to marry him, men want to enter into business relations with him, beggars want to influence him and children want to steal from him. With money's help he survives a death threat in an attempt to enter a nominally closed cult ceremony, yet he grows increasingly uneasy with the ways race and cash merge, as he is indelibly marked as both "profoundly white" and "profoundly wealthy." He is struck, in particular, by the ways money shapes all his fieldwork experiences, from his relations with his closest "informant," to his conversations with wealthy expatriate youth; money mediates, grants power, confers identity. Conversely, during his fieldwork several years later in Berlin, he is stripped of his anthropological aura. Working in one of the most expensive research sites in the world, he finds his research frustrated because he is so strapped for funds. Eventually, however, he finds that the very lack of money allows him to cultivate relations of empathy among members of the repatriated German immigrant community, many of whom are better off than he. The essay points to money's role in shaping field relationships and in configuring research experience at both the micro and macro levels, and it reminds readers of the important role played by wealth in establishing practical ethnographic authority.

These essays show some of the unsettling ways appearances matter. In the field, foreignness is inescapably encoded by wealth and race, a durable association that Senders escaped only by conducting his ethnographic research in Berlin among people who had, ironically, more access to official channels of distribution than did he. Yet the encoding of foreignness and its corollary of wealth is not merely a matter of birth. The focus on money brings with it a concern with mobility and migration, and across the essays we find the movement of people, including anthropologists. As Naeem Inayatullah muses in the final essay, what counter-circulation balances the movement of people?

Money as a Creative Force

Money embodies potential cultural transformation. As a nearly universal object of desire, money has the power to shape and motivate a wide variety of human actions, and therefore to transform practices of interest to anthropologists. The particular ways people spend money – what they do with it and how they do it – frequently serve as an important form of political and personal identification. Money is a critical medium in which people determine, define, act out and reference their identifications. In "Circuits of Conversion," Naeem Inayatullah examines how value, especially monetary value, is place-based, even as his concept of the encounter defies a single location.

Inayatullah, in an essay that intertwines childhood memories, newspaper clippings and conversations with would-be migrants, destabilizes the idea of "the field" as a place. He relates, at one point, a small exchange with a vendor at the airport in Islamabad. The most profound moment of encounter, he confesses, was his hesitation to hand over 400 rupees in change. He traces his shifting relationships with others via money over time, from his glee as a child finding soft drinks bottles along the railroad tracks to his return to Pakistan as a professional scholar employed in the United States. Drawing on the morbid monetary compensation to the victims of 9/11 in New York City and those of an ill-fated air raid in Iraq, he questions money's capacity for expressing human value. Inayatullah's essay is the least conventional in the volume, and in its metaphoric leaps and unexpected connections it poses readers a challenge: How is knowledge that is produced in the instability of encounter to be expressed rhetorically? If we are to produce our own knowledge as readers, the essay implicitly asks, how tightly can we afford to cling to familiar and authorized literary form?

Given the risk posed by monetary exchanges, how then can anthropologists make visible the conditions under which their claims to knowledge are produced? How, in other words, does one secure meaning? The essays in this volume expose anthropologists' anxiety over the possibility of establishing meaningful relations across difference; the danger is that meaning is already a commodity and available for purchase. The anxiety surrounding monetary exchanges, as suggested in these essays, is palpable. Sometimes the anxiety is *ethical*: Have I done the right thing? Have I, as a person of relative wealth, done enough? Has or will my actions damage[d] existing relationships? Sometimes it is *epistemological*: Has my action damaged the quality of my knowledge? Is it "proper" for a "social scientist" to engage in this kind of relationship? In order to make sense of such concerns, we must return to, and represent, the uncertainty of meaning that arises out of particular encounters.

Where do we locate agency in exchange relations when the force of money is so compelling that *everything* is up for sale? How is money itself a creative force for anthropological knowledge? Anthropologists, seeking intimacy, may bring into being new forms of exchange, signified in part by the foreign currency they carry and the kinds of fantasies organized around those currencies. Yet as the essays in this volume demonstrate, anthropologists do not always succeed in either finding or creating the intimacy they seek. The authors of these essays, well aware of their uncertainty, draw on the ironic mode to describe moments of embarrassment, danger and intimacy that stand distinct from theories of indifference that characterize the marketplace. Such indeterminacy propels anthropologists to rationalize and interpret, to analyze and understand, to *do* anthropology. And it is such indeterminacy that makes anthropology unique in its viewpoint, a viewpoint that is simultaneously *current* and *rich*.

CHAPTER 1

Equation Fixations

On the Whole and the Sum of Dollars in Foreign Exchange

Julie Y. Chu

There were many things I expected to find difficult about fieldwork in China but money matters was not one of them. As a graduate student used to stretching the dollar to its limits while living on meager financial aid in one of the world's most expensive cities – New York – I was hopeful that, for once, the elasticity of the dollar would work in my favor. Nothing seemed more clear-cut and alluring about living in China than the promise of my newly expanded purchasing power via the currency exchange rate: 8 Chinese *reminbi* (RMB) to 1 U.S. dollar (USD). This magical equation of 8:1 was, after all, the veritable mantra of the U.S.-bound migrants in Longyan village with whom I was residing and investigating in Fuzhou, China. When I would ask people why they risked life and limb to travel clandestinely through hazardous human smuggling networks to reach the U.S., no phrase was drilled into me more instinctively and repetitively than these three succinct words: *ba bi yi* (8 to 1). U.S. dollars, everyone added, were plainly "bigger" (*bijiao da*) and therefore "better" (*bijiao hao*) than the local Chinese currency. The good life seemed like a no-brainer: get USD, spend RMB.

Given this simple formula, I expected that as a possessor of dollars in China, I would surely be in command of the art of shopping like I had never been before on the tony streets of Manhattan. With the power of 8:1, I was ready to have the world of consumption at my exclusive beck and call in China. My reprieve from penny-pinching, however, did not turn out to be quite as relaxing and rewarding as I imagined. Meager dollars may have converted into more plentiful RMB but, as I discovered, purchasing power turned out to be much more than a numbers game of exchange rates.

My initiation into the toil and turmoil of shopping occurred early on during my fieldwork in Fuzhou when I found myself being angrily chased by a vendor for a good twenty minutes through a sprawling flea market – all because of my accidental, split-second flirtation with one of the items for sale in her stall. In this case, the item in question was a pink T-shirt silk-screened with a squiggly, cartoon graphic of what appeared to be the ghostly sidekicks of Pac-Man (yes, that yellow icon of video games). What had really caught my eye and caused me to linger over this T-shirt was the bouncing English slogan bordering the image of the Pac-Man gang: something incomprehensibly exclamatory ending with "Dance Dance Disco Fun!" Unbeknownst to me at that time, my brief contemplation and chuckle at this T-shirt had roused the previously indifferent vendor out of her torpor. When I thoughtlessly yanked at the shirt to show Liyan – my Chinese friend shopping with me – the humor in it all, things took a decidedly unfunny turn. Inadvertently, I had set the combative ritual of buying and selling in motion.

It started simply enough.

"Miss, this is all cotton. I'll give it to you for just fifty RMB," the vendor announced as she sidled up to us.

"All cotton, it's a very good price, *very good*," she informed us.

"Oh, uh, sorry." I automatically translated my standard browsing-but-not-buying English pleasantry into Chinese.

"I'm just looking … um, *buhao yisi* [pardon me]," I added for humble and polite Chinese effect.

I gestured to my friend Liyan for us to move on to another stall and thought that would be the end of our market repartee over this T-shirt. But as we turned and took our first few steps away from the vendor, she began to wave her hand and the shirt at us with ever more exaggerated and disappointed gestures.

"All right, all right – forty RMB, forty RMB. You can have it for forty," she told us gruffly, as she followed us out of her stall.

"Really, we don't want it." I told her as firmly and clearly as I could, as Liyan and I continued to walk briskly away from her.

"This is real cotton! Go elsewhere and look!" She jabbed her finger at us with indignity. "You can't find better quality for the price! Thirty-five – that's the lowest I can give you – it's almost giving it away!"

"I already told you," I impatiently shot back. "I really, *really* don't want it."

"What do you mean you don't want it? Thirty-five isn't low enough?" the vendor asked.

"All right, all right! Thirty then," the vendor proclaimed. "But *that's* the last of it! What, you won't even let me break even?!"

At this point we had gone a good block and a half around the flea market with this woman stalking us with her insistent haggling and T-shirt in hand for all the other vendors and shoppers to see. Clearly puzzled by my increasingly visible frustration, Liyan pulled me aside.

"What are you thinking? It's not a bad price and she might even go down to twenty," my friend told me.

Liyan, of course, was right about the price. Hell, at the original 50RMB the T-shirt was a *steal* when I thought about it in terms of the exchange rate. Yet all the magic of 8:1 seemed beside the point and could not make me feel better as a shopper at the moment. For somehow Liyan had interpreted my failure at communicating *"no"* to the vendor as a skillful ploy for getting the lowest possible price. Who knew my ineptitude could look so calculated?

Exasperated, I tried explaining again: "When I say, I don't want it, *I mean, I-don't-want-it!*" I told my friend, shaking my head vigorously for extra emphasis. How could I be more explicit?

Convincing Liyan, unfortunately, did nothing to shake the persistent vendor, who wedged the T-shirt between us once more with increasing drama and rancor. As I realized way too late, there was no such thing as "just looking" to Chinese vendors like this woman at the flea market. The act of looking was never neutral, just something one did with no strings attached in the course of shopping in Fuzhou. To linger over an object, as I did with this T-shirt, was to invest it with consumer desire and potential market value. It was an invitation to the ritual of haggling, with all its implied drama of offers and counter-offers. Once I had accidentally signaled my interest in the T-shirt to the vendor, walking away and repeatedly saying "no" could easily be read as part of the theatrics of bargaining. So even as we had walked two and a half aisles away from the vendor's original booth, she continued to trail us while hurling prices and insults with equal vigor.

"Geesh [*zhenshi*]!" Liyan finally huffed on my behalf when she realized we were unable to shake this vendor.

"She said she didn't want it so why don't you go back to your store?" Liyan tried to reason with her.

"She doesn't want it?! Then why waste my time?" the vendor complained. "What, Miss, it isn't good enough? Go look around then!" she demanded. "I tell you, go and see if you can find better here! Go then! *Go look! Go, go, go!*"

The vendor was beside herself with our perceived insults and injuries to all her efforts and her goods. But she had yet to call it quits. Even after a solid ten-minute walk she still stuck to us like an embarrassing "kick me" note on the back. After a while, I started to wonder if I would *ever* shake this vendor without agreeing to buy her goods. Would she follow me out of this market and all the way home just to yell at me about this T-shirt while I proceeded to cook and eat dinner? Would I wake up tomorrow morning only to find her continuing the harangue – But it's pure cotton! – while I brushed my teeth? In a paranoid and desperate moment, I thought of succumbing to the sale just to get her off my back. Perhaps if I convinced myself that this was all about the 8:1 exchange rate, it wouldn't be so bad to lose 30RMB. Somehow, though, I knew I would still feel like a fool – whether a 30-RMB fool or a 5-USD fool.

Alas, it took more than twenty minutes and a couple more blocks around the flea market before we thought we had freed ourselves – *finally* – from this vendor. In fact, we had just recovered our composure enough for some intentional haggling over an umbrella I truly wanted to buy when there she was again, stomping towards us once more, with that Pac-Man T-shirt still in her hand. There was no other choice: I dropped the umbrella, grabbed Liyan's arm and headed for the nearest exit.

"No more shopping," I told my friend in exhausted defeat.

"All right, then. Let's go," Liyan sighed in resignation.

"That woman was really something. A true nutcase [*shenjing bing*]," my friend muttered with a faint wisp of bemusement, quietly chuckling to herself about our shopping debacle.

Shortly after this incident, Liyan decided to accompany me once more on my quest to purchase an umbrella after the last one had been so unceremoniously dropped in mid-haggle in my moment of panic at the flea market. Considering the 8:1 exchange rate, I knew I could probably get a good deal – at least, dollar-wise – with or without my friend by my side. But this time I was determined to feel like a savvy, or at least self-respecting, shopper by following Liyan's lead in the rules of consumer engagement. A no-nonsense Chinese native, Liyan promised to be a model of purchasing power on this shopping venture by serving as my surrogate in the art of the haggle or what the locals called *taojia huanjia* (literally, solicit price, return price). Whatever I wanted to buy, she would negotiate on my behalf and in the process, hopefully, show me the ropes in this still unfamiliar and intimidating world of money talk and commodity exchange.

This time around we headed to Student Row, the ever-jammed and festive commercial strip hugging the hillside of a teacher's college and nearby secondary schools on the southern edge of the city. Up this winding, frantic street of shops, we pushed our way through roving, arm-linked cliques of fresh-faced school girls in baggy gym uniforms and preening teenage boys with matching bleached hair and bellbottom jeans, all the while avoiding eye contact with the aggressive salespeople trying to draw attention with blaring blow horns in their hands. By then, I had learned how unintended looks and careless browsing could get one into trouble. So we studiously made a beeline for the first accessories and knick-knack store in our sight.

After scouring the aisles past the piles of Hello Kitty vinyl wallets, sparkly butterfly hairclips and Taiwanese pop-star stationary, we finally zeroed in on a bin of assorted umbrellas gathering dust near the foot of the cashier's counter. Sifting through this bin, Liyan and I weighed each umbrella between us for its relative value – gripping the handle of one umbrella for its comfort and weight, sliding open another for its relative ease and coverage. Ultimately, the question before us boiled down to this: was there one umbrella out of this bunch that was worth haggling over? For as with all goods at the flea market, there were no monetary figures on display, no visible price tags on anything in this store. No cost of purchase could be determined without first engaging the seller in some fierce rounds of *taojia huanjia*. The price would have to be hard fought and hard won. It would have to be *work*.

Just as Liyan and I thought we had found an umbrella worth fighting for, a sprightly young woman, not more than late teens, launched the opening shot.

"Miss, you want that? It's on sale right now," she told us. "A great price ..."

I stepped aside to leave Liyan with the umbrella and the next move in her hands.

"How much?" my friend asked coolly.

"Twenty-four RMB – it's twenty percent off. Used to be thirty," the teenager replied with confidence.

"What? How could this *count* as a discount? *So* expensive!" Liyan jumped a small step back as if shocked by some lewd insult.

The theatrics of haggling had begun.

"That's our best price, Miss," the young saleswoman held firm.

Liyan responded by inspecting the umbrella in her clutched hand with equal parts of perplexity and disdain.

"No way!" she cried out in disbelief. "How could it be this much? The material is just average. It's not even anything good … One to two years and it'll break!" Liyan predicted. "Ten RMB – can't be more than ten RMB!"

Although the umbrella seemed perfectly fine when we picked it out of the bin just minutes before, Liyan now acted as if it might crumble in her hand with the slightest of motions.

"Miss, you're really mistaken," the sales clerk admonished Liyan with sadness in her voice. "This umbrella of ours is the same as the ones sold in Fuzhou's *most* expensive department stores. No difference except ours is cheaper. If you don't believe me, go look for yourself," the clerk challenged my friend.

After Liyan heaped a new round of scornful looks and insults on the umbrella in question and the teenager responded with a new set of indignation, finally, the price began to budge.

"Look, this is the best I can do," the clerk noted as she furiously tapped a calculator with the tip of a pen and then insolently tossed it Liyan's way with a final figure: 20RMB.

Liyan snorted at the number and shot back another number, "Twelve RMB."

The sales clerk silently shook her head and crossed her arms in steely defiance.

After what seemed like an interminable pause, Liyan tried again.

"All right, all right. Fourteen then … fourteen then …" she repeated the number briskly and decisively as she began to pull some bills out of her wallet.

"Take it, take it then," Liyan gruffly ordered the teenager, as she disdainfully pushed the money her way without once looking the sales clerk in the face.

For a brief but pointed moment, the clerk did not move or respond in silent protest over her maltreatment by Liyan. Then with an equally efficient gesture, she snapped the money out of Liyan's hand and then, without a word, stomped away from us to the cashier's counter. After listening with a determined scowl and downcast eyes to the fading footsteps of the sales clerk, Liyan finally nudged me with a friendly elbow and broke into a conspiratorial, victorious smile. I sighed in relief: it looked like the rough and tense tussle over money had finally reached its conclusion.

As it turned out, I was wrong to think that a settled *price* would be the end of money matters between buyer and seller. When the sales clerk returned with change for Liyan, my friend again grew hostile while scrutinizing a crumpled 2RMB bill she had been handed.

"What's the idea?!" she angrily confronted the teenager. "Why'd you give me money this worn-out and damaged [*po*]! Go get me another!" Liyan impatiently demanded as she tossed the ragged 2RMB note back to the sales clerk.

Not budging from her spot, the teenager rolled her eyes. "Money's money," she shrugged indifferently. "This old bill – we also got it from a customer, so now we pass it back to a customer … If *you* don't want it, it's not *our* problem," the clerk added.

"*What?!*" Liyan was apoplectic at this point. "Money this old, this damaged – *where* can you possibly *use* it?" Liyan asked. "Tell me, who else is going to accept it, huh? *Who else?!* How can you give people this kind of useless change?" she scolded the clerk. "You call *this* doing *business?*"

Exasperated and weary, the sales clerk heaved a low sigh and finally tossed a brand-new, crisp 2RMB bill Liyan's way to stop her from ranting. While Liyan was finally appeased by this exchange, she stood in the store for a few minutes more while suspiciously inspecting another brand-new 50RMB bill that the same sales clerk had handed to her as change.

"A lot of new bills out there are also fake," she explained as she showed me how to rub a finger against the grain of the bill to feel for its proper inked texture and then to fold it in halves and thirds to check for the correct alignment of watermarks.

I came out of this experience feeling more intimidated than ever about shopping in China. Not only did one need to brace for some hostile exchanges of looks, insults and money talk in order to seal a deal, it seemed that the actual bills changing hands in the end were themselves full of suspicion and potential deceit. Nothing seemed transparent or secure when it came to the exchange of money for goods – neither the price of the commodity nor the money used in payment. From the initial act of haggling to the final transaction of purchase, one constantly fought against the demoralizing feeling of being outsmarted and duped by a craftier seller armed with uncanny, high-ball prices and worthless, fake money for change. A raw deal, as I learned, was never just a matter of monetary loss but, moreover, an inescapable reflection of one's character and moral worth.

I never did develop a knack for shopping, despite the best efforts of friends like Liyan in schooling me in the art of the haggle and the science of counterfeit bills. Perhaps I was just too attached or too stubborn to give up my American expectations of "shopping": the sense of anonymity and private space, the trained smiles of "customer service," the various comforts of standardization from price tags to muzak. For despite my earlier fantasies of superior purchasing power in China, shopping became a singular source of personal stress and embarrassment in my everyday life. This was mainly because people never ceased to look at me with profound disappointment whenever I failed to haggle fiercely enough for a better price or when I blithely accepted worn-out and crisply new bills without much angry protest or careful examination. In fact, the combative pressure of *taojia huanjia* ultimately made me avoid shopping as much as possible and, when necessary, to purchase things stealthily outside the protective, familiar circle of pitying friends.

Truth be known, I became a bona-fide secret over-payer in China, meekly accepting sky-high opening offers from stunned proprietors who had been gearing up for a good money fight. To me, it never seemed to be worth the hassle to haggle a vendor over a few RMB here and there – particularly when I converted the amounts into pennies and nickels in USD. But to those around me, to fixate on the numerical sum of monetary equations was to miss out on the *whole* of monetary exchange. Purchasing power was less about how much money one could spend than about how skillfully one negotiated exchange relations in the act of sealing a deal. The best price, after all, was worth fighting for because in the ritual of *taojia huanjia*, it was always business *and* personal at the same time. In money matters these two aspects could not be separated.

While it has often been suggested that money is an impersonal medium of exchange, the transcendent equivalent of all things, yet not quite a "thing" in itself, I could not help but notice the plainness and simple materiality of the money changing hands in the countless shopping transactions I witnessed and personally bungled through during my time in Fuzhou. Watching Liyan, among others, tossing back ragged, old RMB notes and rubbing the inked watermarks on crisp new ones with equal suspicion, I learned to appreciate money for its particular sensual properties as various paper bills and metal coins and for its personal and social meanings as distinctive state currencies – as RMB and as USD. In fact, despite my laziness and general distaste for inspecting every RMB I got for signs of counterfeit, people's anxieties over the trustworthiness of their currency did ultimately have an infectious effect on me. For instance, it affected not only where I changed currency (only at reputable branches of the Bank of China) but moreover, how closely I examined my newly acquired stack of RMB when I did so. Moreover, like others in possession of USD around me, I learned to exchange USD only sparingly, obtaining only what RMB was necessary to meet my monthly expenses.

While 8:1 may have been the instinctive slogan of the U.S.-bound Fuzhounese migrants, as I found out, it was not the only reason people thought dollars were "bigger" and "better." If RMB changed hands amidst plenty of mutual scrutiny and suspicion, the opposite was true of dollars, which usually flowed smoothly from one party to another with much confidence and trust. This is partly because, while people used RMB in everyday market transactions among strangers they had no reason to trust, they mainly circulated USD as remittances, loans or gifts to already familiar others such as kin, friends and neighbors.[1] RMB, as people told me, was the currency they "spent" and used to "buy things," whereas USD were strictly for giving and receiving in intimate circles and on special occasions. In contrast to the combative tit-for-tat of RMB exchanges, where people eyed the money and goods changing hands with equal suspicion, the practical handling of dollars was often quite one-sided, if mutually affirmative, among the villagers with whom I lived in the Fuzhou countryside. Regardless of whether it was a loan from a neighbor or repayment to gods at local temples, the giver typically did all the counting and handling of dollars, while the receiver humbly and unquestioningly accepted the money. I was often impressed by the giver, who under the purview of the recipient, would briskly shuffle through the stack of money with the efficiency of a bank teller and the bravado of a card player. In turn, the recipient would quickly stow away the stack of bills without inspection or care as if embarrassed by any suggestion of suspicion or calculation. Unlike RMB transactions, to scrutinize the USD changing hands in these circumstances was to undermine the very foundation of personal trust through which such monetary exchange could occur in the first place.

But there was yet a larger reason why villagers invested so much more trust in the USD over the RMB. As I discovered, the same suspicion of unfair gain that tainted all my shopping ventures was also echoed in village gripes about local officials and party elites, who just happened to be seen by villagers as the main beneficiaries of RMB wealth. Specifically, people often complained that the wealth made locally by officials and village elites involved unfair advantages like better access to higher education and superior personal connections. Moreover, there was widespread suspicion that RMB wealth was produced by dishonest means, such as embezzlement, bribery, favoritism and other corrupt practices involving the abuse of political authority. After all, if no secret corruption existed behind the accumulation of RMB, people reasoned, then why was all the Chinese state's currency ending up mainly in the hands of those with privileged state positions? In turn, why did the efforts of honest and hard-working commoners not result in local prosperity? In contrast to the suspicious fortunes of local elites, the meager earnings of internal migrants from the hinterlands of China were often cited as evidence of the futility of honest labor as a means to RMB accumulation. Everyone may have some RMB to spend and to lose but, as most villagers complained, only officials and local elites seemed to have it in *excess*.

This is why the goal of getting USD to spend RMB made both practical *and* moral sense to these outward-bound Fuzhounese villagers. For unlike the RMB, the dollar provided Longyan residents with an alternative means for imagining money accumulation as a morally earned and therefore deserving project. While the suspect RMB wealth of officials and elites only seemed to reinscribe a status quo of local inequality, dollar prosperity suggested that through the alienating and challenging trials of honest labor abroad, the most humble commoners could be transformed into the successful entrepreneurial vanguard of a new Chinese modernity. Elaborately displayed in temple rituals and other local festivities, dollars were powerful tokens of a rite of passage through which Fuzhounese villagers imagined transforming themselves from marginal "peasants" into model cosmopolitans. Not only did the USD have the superior exchange value of 1:8 RMB, but through the process of its accumulation overseas, the dollar, unlike the RMB, also offered a success story premised on a moral ethos of hard work and sacrifice. In this way, saying that the dollar was "bigger" and "better" than the RMB was never just a declaration of monetary value but also a judgment of the moral value of those who held such different currencies.[2]

Notes

1. Unlike the RMB, the USD was never used for commercial purchases in Fuzhou. Rather, it mainly changed hands through personal circles as markers of success overseas, affirmation of social ties or as extensions of personal credit. The one exception to this intimate sphere of exchange is the national banking institution which generally mediated the overseas transfers of USD from relatives abroad to villagers in Fuzhou as well as the exchange of USD for RMB (along with the local black market for currency exchange, which could also be considered a sphere of intimate relations). Typically, people would exchange USD for RMB only as needed for making everyday market transactions, which only took place with RMB as the currency of exchange. It is also important to mention that people give monetary gifts not only in USD but also sometimes in RMB, though for reasons I mention below in this paper, USD gifts are preferred because of the superior moral associations of this currency.

2. While the moral discourse of RMB wealth revolves around suspicions of state corruption, I have noted elsewhere how villagers with dollar wealth are sometimes accused of "wastefulness" and "selfishness." However, corruption does not seem to figure at all in moral complaints against those with overseas wealth.

CHAPTER 2

Changing Money in Post-Soviet Ukraine

J. A. Dickinson

When the Soviet Union dissolved in 1991, it left behind a collection of "successor states," each needing its own new symbols of legitimacy. Gone from these states' new currencies was the iconic image of Lenin, but what could replace it? In post-Soviet Ukraine, consumers (myself the ethnographer among them) endured years of turbulent economic change before this question was answered in 1996, with the introduction of a new national currency, the *hryvnia*. In this unsettled period, changing money played such a central role in my field experiences that I could not help but realize how closely bound economics, identity and language were in the rapidly changing world of post-Soviet Ukraine. The promise of a national currency was not just about the credibility of the post-Soviet Ukraine government; it was also about the meaning of change symbolically expressed in valuations of the many currencies circulating in the markets, in people's memories of the past and their visions of the future.

While governments negotiated the design of new money, people in the former Soviet Union, and indeed all over Eastern and Central Europe, were engaging with the market and commercial goods in ways that contrasted sharply with their lives under socialism (Verdery 1996, Humphrey 2002). Buying things, and buying the right things, became a lightening rod for cultural expression – whether of "normalcy," as Rausing (2004) argues for a rural Estonian village; a sign of economic identity, as Berdahl (1999) suggests for East Germans after the reunification of Germany; or a statement of national pride, as Caldwell (2002) discusses for Moscovites' food purchases. Everyday acts of purchasing, provisioning and planning continued to be everyday acts, yet the spaces and means by which they were accomplished were constantly being evaluated, criticized, embraced and argued over. Against this backdrop of economic, cultural and social reorganization, the experiences I discuss in this article can be understood as moments where the meaning of money stepped into the foreground, highlighting these unruly processes of change in the Ukrainian context.

The Exchange Booth, 1993

In post-Soviet Ukraine of the early 1990s, trade in foreign currencies, illegal during the Soviet period, burst from the back alleys of the black market into the shadowy spaces of the "gray" economy. Suddenly, ordinary citizens could legally buy or sell dollars, marks and, even more jarring, new *Russian* rubles in the broad daylight of government-sanctioned exchange kiosks. Traders ensconced in these booths, which stood alone on the street or were tucked into faded Soviet-era stores selling fabrics or school-supplies, often experienced brisker commerce than people selling "real" goods. Particularly in the first months and years after Ukrainian independence, it sometimes seemed that few people had money to buy anything but food and stable currencies like U.S. dollars.

For me, the anthropologist, the exchange booth played a key role in my entrance into the daily life of post-Soviet Ukraine. On my first day back in Kiev since the breakup of the Soviet Union, I slid my dollars through the small hatch at the front of one such kiosk and received a pile of little white Ukrainian banknotes in return. "Monopoly money," I thought to myself, walking away as I shuffled a bunch of the bills emblazoned with the word *kupon* ("coupon") and variously printed in shades of green, blue, orange, purple and pink. The bills were about the size of a sheet of play money from that quintessentially capitalist board game. To most of the people shuffling along the cold gray winter street beside me, the bills were more evocative of the smallest of the Soviet banknotes, the one-ruble bill, which the *kupony* matched exactly in size.

The kupony were my "ticket" into the daily economic life of post-Soviet Ukraine, yet my reaction to them was deeply embedded in my own cultural notions of what money should be. I fingered the stiff paper of a crisp 5-kupon note and decided it lacked whatever transformed mere paper into money: it had pretty pictures on the front and back, but no serial number; the paper was too smooth, heavy rather than flexible. I doubted it would wear well, and indeed another bill in my stack, issued less than a year before, was almost torn in two where it had been folded, and its edges were frayed and fuzzy. "This," I thought, "is the currency of a country teetering on the edge …" then quickly suppressed that surge of ethnocentric chauvinism, the feeling that "their" money didn't measure up to "ours."

A few doors down from the exchange kiosk, I stepped into a small store to buy bread, but when I tried to pay with that torn and faded note, the cashier handed it back to me with a firm, "I won't take this one." With her rejection, my initial doubt turned into suspicion mixed with ethnographic curiosity. Perhaps I wasn't alone in my unease with this currency.

Over the course of that visit and return trips to the field, I gradually realized that while Ukrainians did not call the interim currency "play money," they, too, had doubts about it. As these "coupons" moved in and out of their hands in day-to-day life, as they used the word kupon again and again, I began to understand that many of them were wondering, just as I was, when the new currency for the newly independent nation would arrive. As spiraling inflation rapidly devalued the kupon, the date for introducing the real currency was pushed back further and further. The shifting exchange rates were a barometer of contemporary economic conditions and future prospects of the newly independent Ukrainian state.

An Urban Market, Uzhhorod, 1995

When I returned to the field in the summer of 1995 to begin a new project in the southwestern border region of Zakarpattia,[1] the "interim" kupon was still serving as the official Ukrainian currency, but the once-flimsy bills had evolved into something more substantial and complex. They were larger and had the sophisticated look and feel a "real" currency. Inflation had long since done away with the quaint three- and five-kupon notes, and this time I received a stack of 100,000-kupon bills, and even a 1,000,000-kupon denomination, when I stopped at an exchange booth. "I'm a millionaire!" I had heard friends joke when they received their monthly wages, and when I asked my friend Marina how she felt about the new bills, she told me that her friends sometimes playfully referred to *limony* (lemons) instead of *miliony* (millions). The word kupon was such a part of daily life that it no longer seemed ironic to do business using a temporary currency originally intended to circulate for only a few months. Instead, these jibes about millions and lemons focused everyone's attention, including mine, on the sour gap between early hopes of earning millions of dollars from the new capitalist market economy, and the reality of not being able to afford several million kupon to buy a pair of jeans.

Money was a ready topic of conversation with the people I met. Like many ethnographers working in the former Soviet Union during this period, I frequently participated in illegal or semi-legal currency exchanges, from "selling" dollars to friends for less than the established legal rate, or using coded questions to inquire about the dollar (not kupon) price of an item at the market. Learning the codes of these interactions required a combination of observation, trial and error, and sometimes explicit instruction by friends who accompanied me to the *bazar* (market), and even the traders themselves.

In the city of Uzhhorod, my cultural tutor in these matters was most often my friend Marina, who had briefly worked at the local "thing" market to supplement her university salary. Unlike produce and meat markets, which had been an accepted and legal part of the Soviet distribution system, the resale of other goods were the purview of newly legalized "thing" markets, at which everything from makeup to clothing and television sets was sold. In 1995, the Uzhhorod bazar consisted of a crowded double-ring of tiny stalls filling the soccer stadium, ousting the local team benched by lack of funds. Similar to many such places throughout the former Soviet Union, the bazar was loud and hectic, and the atmosphere was thick with tension peculiar to "thing" markets. While the slim profit margins and established rules of the produce markets were socially accepted, I quickly surmised the conventional wisdom on "thing" markets in Uzhhorod: they were full of profit-hungry thieves, dishonest merchants and people with criminal ties.

When I finally took my first trip to "the stadium," as this local market was called, I immediately sensed the tension: while the sellers remained wary, poised to react at the first sign of tax police or thieves, the customers were also on guard, always alert to being swindled or shortchanged. People expressed their anxieties about the newly legal status of selling goods for profit, and their own ambivalence about working in public markets. These activities had been criminalized as "speculation" during the Soviet period. Now, as new laws and taxes shaped Ukraine's post-socialist economy, sellers never knew, which side of the law they would find themselves. At the same time, customers often harbored a deep distrust of middlemen who "earned money from other people's labor," as one man I interviewed characterized it.

Although I didn't share this distrust of private enterprise per se, I did find myself heeding friends' warnings about money. They feared my U.S. dollars would attract unwanted attention, that as an American I would be overcharged, pick-pocketed or sold bad merchandise. As I walked around the rows of stalls with Marina, thinking about the dollars and kupon bills I had tucked away, I drew a sense of security from Marina's familiarity with the market layout and her personal acquaintance with particular sellers, which served as a buffer against the threat of deception.

One day I wanted to buy a pair of gold earrings for my mother. Several people had told me to avoid buying "cheap" Turkish gold that had been smuggled into the country, and instead to buy "local" jewelry still believed to be purer and of higher quality. Marina explained that items produced in factories had a *proba*, a stamp certifying the quality of the gold, the same stamp that had been used to mark quality in the Soviet Union. Although faith in the stamp might be misplaced, it functioned to guarantee the quality of gold, which remained valuable despite the economic upheavals and rapidly escalating kupon denominations of the past four years.

Once Marina and I agreed that, stamp or no stamp, gold would be cheaper at the bazar than in the store, we headed to the stadium where we entered the throng of customers and sellers, weaving our way along the narrow path between the booths. Suddenly, Marina pulled me aside, stopping in front of a man standing behind a small table filled with socks, underwear and hairclips. Although he had no jewelry on display, Marina assured me in a stage whisper that he sold gold. She approached him with the claim that an acquaintance had told her he might have some other goods to sell that were not on display. Reluctantly, he pulled out a small pouch with several pieces of gold jewelry in it. As I selected the earrings, Marina asked him which factory the jewelry had come from. The seller replied, but glanced around nervously for the tax police. I asked how much the item I wanted cost, and he quoted me a kupon price. Marina then leaned in and casually said *"A esli drugimi?"* ("And how about with other [money]?"). He named a dollar price based on a better exchange rate than I would find at any bank in town. As I pulled out some folded dollars, he became visibly more nervous. "What are you doing?" he scolded me for showing the dollars in the open, and he quickly covered the money with his hand as he took it from me.

The man's reaction refocused my attention on the anxieties of the market and on the strikingly different roles of two currencies, the dollar and kupon, in the market (see Lemon 1998 and Pine 2002). His rebuke, and the rush of adrenaline it brought, taught me an important lesson – U.S. dollars must be hidden. After this encounter, I fell into the habit of circumspectly slipping dollars from my palm to a seller's each time I returned to the field. When I moved to a village to do fieldwork, I took this lesson with me, but found I still had a great deal more to learn about the meaning of money in Zakarpattia.

A Village Market, Zakarpattia Region, 1995 and 1996

Any threads of monetary understanding I had gathered turned into a tangled knot when I settled into a village about five hours' drive from Uzhhorod. In this context, I was a novelty, a precious trinket to be protected from a wide range of perils that ranged from sickness brought on by the "evil eye" to being "kidnapped," whether for ransom or to be sold into white slavery, I was never quite sure. At night, my host family let loose their guard dog in the yard, effectively preventing anyone from leaving the house until the family matriarch corralled him in the morning. Not surprisingly, they too cautioned me about the dangers of the bazar. They were particularly afraid I might trade my U.S. dollars with the currency traders, or *valiutchyky*. While at first I chafed against what I perceived as over-protectiveness, I later came to understand their efforts to protect me reflected how they themselves felt vulnerable to the supernatural, physical and economic dangers of unstable post-Soviet life.

Those pitfalls were more visible to me in this village tucked into the mountains near the Romanian border than they had been in the cities. Here the economy, once supported by outdated factories and struggling collective farms, had stalled. Any prospects for renewal in this village seemed far bleaker than in the cities. In some ways, the village conformed to the classic stereotypes people in larger cities like Kiev and Lviv had invoked in describing Zakarpattia to me. Much of the region is mountainous and land-poor. Elsewhere in Ukraine, people described it as a wild, "backwoods" area where the locals speak an unintelligible dialect and live in conditions little changed by Soviet modernization. It *was* true that there was no running water in the village, people still used horse-drawn carts for most farm work, electricity had arrived relatively recently, and the dialect was so liberally salted with local words and borrowings from nearby Romanian and Hungarian speakers that people from other parts of Ukraine struggled to understand them.

Within a few days I discovered that this undeniable rurality was counterbalanced by a population that was highly mobile within, and even beyond, Europe. Ethnic Romanians and Hungarians traveled across local borders to shop, work and visit with relatives; unemployed workers migrated to Russia, the Czech Republic, the former Yugoslavia and even

Spain or Israel for agricultural, construction and factory jobs. Even people without the cash to buy international passports still migrated to other parts of Ukraine for seasonal work or to buy goods for resale in local markets. For these reasons, the exchange system in rural Zakarpattia evolved in the opposite direction from the demonetized moonshine-based currency system Rogers (2005) describes for parts of Russia. Instead, I found the village saturated with multiple currencies – U.S. dollars,[2] Russian rubles, Polish zlotys, Hungarian forints, German marks and Czech korunas all passed through the hands of valiutchyky, transforming occasionally into Ukrainian kupony, and later, the new *hryvni*.

At that time, the nearest telephone was still three miles away and the nearest bank that could exchange foreign currency legally was a forty-five-minute drive. Yet a pedestrian border crossing into Romania was only a few miles away. With no safe and officially sanctioned exchange booths to rely on, the local population turned to the valiutchyky, who did a profitable business trading kupony for foreign currencies. The valiutchyky were all young men, many contemporaries of my research assistant Natalia (then twenty), and they had all been, she scornfully noted, mediocre students in school, destined in the Soviet period for mundane factory careers. Now, however, the world had turned upside-down and they had somehow ended up literally holding the purse strings, representing the triumph of cagey mediocrity over Soviet-era values of education and production-oriented labor. She pointed them out to me as we walked into the village market. A small group of two or three valiutchyk, eyes shielded by sunglasses and fanny packs full of cash, lounged in the road near the fence between the old market where women sold their own dairy products and mushrooms and the dusty expanse of the new bazar where people sold Turkish-made clothing, Hungarian macaroni and Russian auto parts. Natalia's mother had sternly told her not to let me near the valiutchyky, so I watched from afar as they conducted the business of changing money with studied casualness, in a low voice, leaning together over the primary tool of the money-trading trade, a cheap calculator.[3]

The valiutchyky were villagers, usually familiar with, and sometimes even related to, their customers. At the same time, they were separated by their role as currency traders and their connections to a broad network of marginally legal or criminal activities that ready access to foreign currencies was presumed to entail. At once shadowy and familiar, cast in the role of benevolent con men, they comprised an alternative, parallel economic system that filled in the gaps in rural monetary life where the government banking system couldn't reach (Reis 2002).

As in the city markets, my friends steered me away from encounters with the money changers, insisting that it would be dangerous to reveal that I had U.S. dollars. While I had my doubts about the necessity of this ruse, I abided by my friends' wishes. Whenever I needed to change money in the village, I either asked someone to change money for me, or I approached one of several successful female traders with whom I shared mutual personal trust. While I could have been cast in the role of "*vali-utnystia*,"[4] I cannot remember ever being approached by anyone in the village with a request to sell U.S. dollars for Ukrainian currency.[5] Despite my relative wealth in dollars and my frequent trips to the regional center or other areas of Ukraine, I was not identified as a source of hard currency.

My efforts to comprehend my own role, or lack of a role, in this system of currency exchange led me to a much larger ethnographic project. What were the available economic roles and relationships just emerging or being reconfigured in post-Soviet Ukrainian village life? The effects of migrant labor, the dismantling of the local collective farm, the closing of state enterprises and factories, and the increasing importance of the local bazar were all inextricably bound to issues of money, work and identity. To become a valiutchyk was to take up a position defined only partially by one's access to hard currency; more important was access to broad social networks and a willingness to occupy the liminal space between legitimate and illegal economic activities. This ethnographic exercise of mapping out a range of cultural positions and how relationships to dollars and kupony were implicated in local understandings of each one helped me understand who I was in the village context.

As I interviewed, conversed, and absorbed information about work and economic change in the village, I took on the role of sister, daughter and godmother in a village family. Others in the village who did not know me so well had, unbeknownst to me, affixed me with another, archaic label, as I discovered one day when I overheard a neighbor asking "Would your *panika* [literally, 'little miss'] be able to give us a lift to the market?" While I balked at the word panika, with its overtones of pre-Soviet aristocratic idleness and distance, this label also located my real position in the local system. People knew I was there to do research on village life, but that was a social designation, one that didn't jive with the available economic classifications: I wasn't a state employee or a regular student with a monthly stipend paid in kupony; I wasn't a migrant laborer, because I hadn't brought my dollars back from a temporary job abroad; I wasn't a money changer, because money changers were male and of local origin; I wasn't a trader, because I didn't sell things and wasn't in business. I was a panika, culturally as far from the gray economic world of money changers as one could get, and therefore in need of protection from the economic and social dangers of the bazar.

U.S. dollars in my hands signified something different than dollars in the hands of migrant workers returned from abroad, moneychangers hunched over their calculators in the bazar or workers who purchased hard currency with their wages as a hedge against kupon inflation. In the urban anonymity of the city bazar U.S. dollars were impersonal, but in the village their meaning was inseparable from the person who possessed them. At the same time, people sometimes forgot that dollars were my "native" currency; instead, in the village context dollars functioned as sort of international hard currency, standing in opposition to the local, soft-currency kupon. When the introduction of the "real" Ukrainian national currency was announced in the summer of 1996, I wondered how these different currencies, and what they indexed about peoples' economic and social identities, would shift.

The Money Changes: Zakarpattia, 1996

A few months after my arrival to the village, the Ukrainian National Bank orchestrated the long-awaited introduction of the new Ukrainian currency, the hryvnia, and withdrawal of the now defunct kupon from circulation. I learned about the impending currency change like most people, via the government's intense publicity campaign. For example, the evening news aired a clip from a museum in Kiev of a display of the ancient hryvnia coins after which the new currency was named.

The news stories and government announcements focused on both the symbolic and economic significance of the new currency. Some discussed the ancient roots of the hryvnia in the kingdom of Kievan Rus, which many Ukrainian nationalists argue is the historical predecessor of contemporary independent Ukraine.[6] Along with these historical narratives, the images on the new currency underscored an independent Ukrainian state. The one-hryvnia note carried the image of Vladimir the Great, Kievan Rus' first Christian king. At the same time, the news stories emphasized that the threat of inflation, which had delayed the currency release for several years, was over. Gone with the kupon would be prices in the millions (and those kupon millionaires), as people turned in their old money for new at the exchange rate of 100,000 kupony for one new hryvnia.

The campaign caught my interest as I recalled living in Latvia in 1993 when the new national currency, the *lats*, was released. An air of patriotic excitement surrounded the little exchange booths. People interpreted the currency change as a sign of good things to come, as a happy day in their nation's history. Taking this as a model, I was excited when the village's tiny post-office/bank received an informational poster intended to familiarize people with the new currency by offering an "up close" view of the new money. In addition to pictures of the bills, the poster enumerated the currency's seventeen security features (more, it was pointed out to me, than the contemporary U.S. dollar).[7] I even asked whether I could buy the poster as a souvenir of the historic changeover, but the manager told me very sternly that they would be using it to identify possible forgeries in the months after the introduction of the hryvnia.

Anticipating the same excitement in my friends, I was disappointed by their blasé, even negative attitude towards the hryvnia. In the village, people had regularly bought and sold different currencies for a number of years, all the while cultivating strong opinions about what a "good" currency should look like. Their experiences became the basis for judgments about the Ukrainian government and its economic policies, and the conclusions they reached were often harsh and ripe with dissatisfaction. One woman mocked the Ukrainian national anthem, "Ukraine has Not Yet Died," by noting "No, it is still dying," while another woman joked "A free Ukraine? Free of everything: jobs, food, clothing ..." As villagers complained bitterly about staggering unemployment, unpaid back wages, corruption and legislative stagnation, the government's campaign to promote the historical and patriotic significance of the hryvnia's release fell flat. They griped about the choice of the name hryvnia, pointing out that the kupon was a "coupon for *karbovantsy*," the Ukrainian word for ruble also used during the Soviet period. To them, the resurrection of an ancient currency name over a "perfectly good Ukrainian word" was not a fresh start for the new nation, but rather a calculated blow to the Soviet past that many of them idealized as economically stable, even relatively prosperous, in comparison to their experiences in post-Soviet Ukraine.[8]

The differences in how I interpreted the new currency and how the villagers around me interpreted it signaled a divergence in the value of the hryvnia. I had my own abstract ideas about national symbolism, whereas they saw the new currency reform as a concrete, critical and even dangerous economic event. Indeed, after five years of economic instability, residents viewed the approaching currency reform with outright fear. Some issued dire predictions of impending economic chaos: banks would run out of currency and they would be left, as in the wake of the Soviet Union's breakup, with a worthless currency in their hands. To make this point, my research assistant Natalia even pulled a stack of hundreds of Soviet rubles out of a drawer in her kitchen. Once an enormous sum, the ruble had been so devalued at the end that she hadn't bothered to exchange those notes for kupony, instead stashing them away as a "souvenir." In the face of their anger and fear, my "hryvnia fever" faded. Their disappointment in post-Soviet life and their concerns over the viability of the Ukrainian state had so tainted my friends' expectations for the hryvnia that perhaps no currency name or design would have been readily accepted or widely celebrated, as I had witnessed in Latvia with the introduction of the nationally oriented lats.

A few people I knew looked forward to the introduction of the new currency, which followed quickly on the heels of the newly approved constitution, another sign that Ukraine was finally emerging from "interim" laws and money and becoming an established state. At the same time, these individuals also admitted that the new currency meant that they might never be compensated for their back wages or life savings lost in rapid post-Soviet inflation. In autumn, with the introduction of the new currency, many villagers accepted the bitter truth that the factory and state-sponsored jobs would never return. The hopes and promises of the early post-Soviet period were withdrawn right along with the interim currency. The opposing forces of national pride and disillusionment with the economic realities of post-socialism clashed, and I heard conflicting predictions about the fate of the currency reform, often in the same breath. It was a good thing, it was a bad thing. It would boost the economy, it would mean economic collapse. The conversations went around and around as villagers tried on a range of opinions, preparing themselves for different possibilities as they tried to guess the outcome of this latest round of economic reform.

For some, their worst fears were realized when the hryvnia appeared first in the hands of the village valiutchyky, not the local bank. While the banks were focused on implementing the exchange of old kupon bills for the new hryvnia, some valiutchyky, who had no use for the old banknotes, would only accept dollars in exchange for the new currency. Others made a profit by offering fewer new bills in exchange for the old ones, then driving to a larger city and cashing in old bills at the state-sanctioned exchange rate. Early in the changeover, many areas experienced shortages of the new bills. A rumor quickly spread in the village that a bank in a nearby town had not received any bills, even though the valiutchyky were conspicuously well-stocked and briskly trading currency at a higher rate than the bank. Resentment simmered against the valiutchyky, but also against the state system, which again demonstrated a lack of regard for people living outside major population centers. "They're economizing on us, profiting off us, for their own advantage," my friend Maria said angrily, lumping together the state, the valiutchyky and the corrupt banking officials in a nearby town. The latter, she reported, were rumored to have supplied the money changers with hryvnia bills in advance of the official start date of the currency changeover.

I learned about this speculation second-hand because I was traveling outside the village in early September and did not have to approach a valiutchyk for my first look at the new currency. I returned to the village with samples of the new hryvnia bills, which I had legally acquired at an urban exchange kiosk. Despite the ambivalence towards the currency that I had already experienced leading up to the introduction of the hryvnia, as I passed the money around the family I lived with, I still expected, or perhaps hoped, that they would share my excitement over the currency. I waited for them to enthuse over the fine engraving, the high quality paper and the historical significance of the bills, and to express patriotic pride at this national milestone.

"Well, it's a fine currency, isn't it?" Natalia asked in a neutral tone.

Another woman answered, "Yes, it's nice, very nice."

Then after a brief silence I heard a young woman examining a two-hryvnia bill suddenly exclaim: "Look, they made a mistake right here on the currency! It says '*dvi hryvni*,' not '*dva hryvni*'!"[9]

Were doubts about government competence so pervasive that someone, albeit a teenager, could leap to the conclusion that a basic grammatical error had escaped notice on the national currency? While the rest of the group quickly berated her for her silliness, I understood what she was doing. She had voted "no confidence" (or at least "low") in the abilities of the government that it had issued it. Concerns with the economic ramifications of the currency reform suddenly shifted to a referendum on the government's competency. The currency, rather than a triumphant capstone of economic and political transition, was suddenly a vehicle for criticizing the very government that followed the fall of the Soviet Union.

In the village market a couple of days later, the talk was all about the change, most notably in prices, from which five zeros had been dropped. When I asked a seller a price, she flubbed the grammar, unsure whether the currency was masculine or feminine "*Odyn. Odna?* Whatever it is now …" Over and over I heard people switch between two forms, unsure whether their money was the hryvnia or hryven, and I recalled earlier conversations when people wondered why they hadn't chosen a more familiar name like the *karbovanets*. A businessman told me he had even received an email from the national bank outlining the correct spelling, pronunciation and grammatical usage of the word, evidence that the main problem caused by the introduction of the hryvnia was widespread linguistic, rather than economic, confusion.

Indeed, despite the temporary shortages of new currency, the hryvnia successfully entered into circulation without the wide-scale economic panic that some people had predicted. The elaborate anti-counterfeit measures, the technologies of authenticity employed to guarantee faith in the currency, assured people, even in rural areas, to accept the money in their daily lives in much the same way that they had used the kupony. Nevertheless, I was left wondering why the name printed on the currency left people confused. Was their rejection of the state-chosen name for the currency just a classic example of resistance against the overarching power of the state?

Turning it All Over: Uzhhorod Market, 2002

My interest in the matter may have been shared by the government and language experts, but over the next few months, as I listened to people in Zakarpattia settle into their new habits of using and talking about the new currency, I concluded that most people didn't really care what the currency was called. I heard some people call it the hryvnia, others hryven, still others, Russian speakers, *grivnia*.[10] Some simply avoided calling it anything and just used numbers, like that confused seller in the bazar. Meanwhile, I found myself thinking about it as a linguistic anthropologist, casting these "naming issues" in terms of Bakhtin's (1983) discussion of the struggle between centripetal and centrifugal forces in language, an example of the common people resisting an attempt to impose standard forms from above and stifle natural variations in everyday language use. I saw it as their way of undermining the government's grand narratives of the hryvnia as a symbol of Ukraine's glorious past while not rejecting the currency's economic viability.

Perhaps it was the scorn in the voice of that teenage girl as she said "Look, they made a mistake right here on the currency!" that drew my attention to the lack of faith these people had in their government at that time. Over and over again, people referenced the Soviet past in positive economic terms, remembering and representing it to me, and to each other, as a time of security and even prosperity. Idealizing Soviet life, villagers spoke of full employment, regular salaries, abundant consumer goods, and lower tolerance for corruption. Seen in this light, the government's choice of the name hryvnia was also a rejection of the more Soviet word, ruble, *karbovanets* in Ukrainian. While popular support for the new government was strong after Ukraine achieved independence in 1991, by the time the hryvnia was introduced in 1996, many people I knew were nostalgic for the Soviet past and wary of the Ukrainian future. The new currency name, as unfamiliar as this new post-Soviet territory, didn't sit well with them, and it took some time before they made it their own, settling on one version or another, but not much caring which one the national bank said was "right." Throughout it all, life went on, things were bought and sold, and the valiutchyky did a steady business trading dollar for hryvnia and hryvnia for dollar.

During a return trip to the field several years later, an encounter with a seller in the Uzhhorod bazar brought into focus the scattered impressions of change that I had gathered in the field. Since the first day in Kiev, when my stack of kupony made me think of play money, I had thought of dollar and kupon (and later hryvnia) as exchangeable, but not equivalent. One was stable, the other volatile, one was to be offered to a market seller or valiutchyk surreptitiously, the other used in the open. Implicit in these divisions was a hierarchy that placed the dollar above local currency as more desirable and powerful, each currency reflecting on the status of the government it represented. One day, I was in the market buying a gift for a friend, and as we agreed on a price, I asked, lowering my voice, whether she preferred dollars. Shrugging her shoulders, she answered, "There's no difference." Taking out the sum she had indicated, I extended my hand with its enclosed bill carefully hidden, just as I had learned to do in the Uzhhorod market years before. The seller laughed at my subterfuge, turned my palm and the bills I had clutched in it face up, and told me that they had the hryvnia now, and dollars weren't illegal anymore. Her confidence in her own currency was the best evidence I could have had that change was afoot. No matter what people called it, the hryvnia had come into its own as the currency of a new nation.

Notes

1. Zakarpattia, sometimes referred to as Transcarpathia, is a small southwestern Ukrainian region wedged at the crossroads of Central and Eastern Europe. With the recent expansion of the European Union, it is now surrounded by current or

future EU members, bordering on Poland, Slovakia, Hungary and Romania, but as part of Ukraine, not yet in line to join them. Over the past several hundred years the territory has changed hands frequently, and many older residents still remember Hungarian, Czech, German and then Soviet troops moving through their villages in the first half of the twentieth century. Although it is geographically grouped with other areas that were joined to Ukraine after the Second World War, many consider Zakarpattia "less Ukrainian" than other parts of Western Ukraine, which unlike much of the East is dominated by Ukrainian speakers and is recognized as the base of Ukrainian nationalism.

2. Throughout Eastern Europe, during and after the Soviet period, American dollars were considered the "safest" hard currency. In the village where I worked, men would often send money home from their migrant labor jobs in the form of dollars; their families could then use this money to purchase larger items directly, or exchange it for Ukrainian currency.

3. The calculator rapidly replaced the bulkier abacus in trade areas. This might be explained by mere convenience; however, I also noticed in my later research with market sellers that few market workers had formal training as cashiers before becoming market workers, and therefore didn't have the necessary abacus skills to conduct business quickly. In contrast, many food sellers who had worked within the Soviet system continued to use abacuses in their market work.

4. This is an invented, feminine version of the word "valiutchyk," a profession so masculinized that I don't recall ever hearing a woman referred to as such.

5. In contrast, people I barely knew would stop by the house to ask me to drive them somewhere in my car, sometimes expecting me to cover the cost of gasoline.

6. Russian nationalists, in contrast, tend to claim that Kievan Rus is the precursor of the Russian empire, thus making a competing claim for this same historical territory.

7. Although the interim currency did become more sophisticated over the years, billions of counterfeit kupony were uncovered during the currency exchange, further underscoring the sense that the government was not fully in control of the money supply during the early post-Soviet period.

8. In the early 1990s many Zakarpattia residents I talked to, particularly those in poor rural areas, felt that they had benefited from Soviet rule and were often nostalgic for the stability and relative prosperity of Soviet times. For this reason, people I spoke with not only reminisced about the Soviet past, but also expressed concerns about the role that Ukrainian nationalism would play in the development of the Ukrainian state, worrying that what they perceived as the dominant Zakarpattia ideology of linguistic and ethnic inclusiveness would be threatened by "overzealous" Ukrainian nationalists. Of course, people in the area where I did my research expressed multiple and conflicting opinions about Soviet rule, Ukrainian nationalism, inter-ethnic relations and even their identity as Ukrainians. However, at the time of the currency changeover, Ukrainian nationalism was clearly not as strong in this area as in other parts of Western Ukraine.

9. When my young friend exclaimed that a "mistake" had been printed on the two-hryvnia note, she pointed out the use of the feminine form of the word for "two," *dvi*, where she expected to see the masculine word, *dva*. In other words, she thought that the name of the currency was not the hryvnia, a feminine noun, but rather, the hryven, a masculine noun. Throughout Ukraine, there was considerable initial confusion over whether the currency was named the "hryvnia" or "hryven'" and both the official and "folk" names for the currency persisted for some time after the currency was introduced.

10. The "h" sound is not used in most Russian dialects and Russian speakers will usually substitute "g" when pronouncing Russian versions of Ukrainian words.

CHAPTER 3

Dollars and Dolores in Postwar El Salvador

Ellen Moodie

This is a tale of two encounters in the city of Santa Tecla, El Salvador. It is probably a coincidence that both happened around the time of the *Semana Santa* – Holy Week. It is undoubtedly just by chance that both these passing conversations – with a stranger and a near-stranger – alloyed suffering and money, pain and exchange, just at the moment the Christian tradition commemorates the trade of the death of a holy man for the absolution of the sins of humanity. As I reflect on these events six years later, it is coincidentally close to Easter. Affronted North American news editorialists are raging over Mel Gibson's bloody and very profitable *Passion of the Christ*. The film's dramatic images recalled for me – raised in a white, vaguely Presbyterian home in Indiana – the awe I felt the first time I saw the elaborate reenactment of agony in the Roman Catholic rites surrounding Christian crucifixion and resurrection in Central America.

First Encounter: Cappuccino and Quakers

It is April 1998. I am renting a small concrete-block house with erratic water but dependable light in the walled middle-class neighborhood of Altos de Santa Mónica. Nestled in the lower skirts of the Boquerón (San Salvador) volcano, it was built about a decade earlier, in the late 1980s. Many of my neighbors' houses exhibit varied phases of construction (second floors, garages, extra rooms). Much of the work is funded with remittances, the fluctuating flow of dollars sent by laboring migrant sons and sisters up North.[1]

At the entry to the walled colony, two security guards with long rifles loosely monitor traffic, raising a long wooden barrier for cars. The barrier and walls separate the tidy blocks of homes, our *residencial*, from the marginal *comunidad* Las Margaritas, a long, curved row of brick-and-mud huts and corrugated-metal shacks. Once this slum-like zone sheltered hundreds of coffee *cortadores* (cutters) who, between October and March, came to work the shaded green plantations that covered the region's dark volcanic soil. Occasionally I sense the rotten-sour stench of coffee pulp here. (And in those moments I flash back to my bourgeois-bohemian post-college years in Hoboken, New Jersey, where the richer aroma of roasting beans sometimes wafted down Washington Street from the Maxwell House plant. Manhattanites might remember the neon coffee cup, flashing "Good to the last drop," across the Hudson until about 1992. The plant's corporate owners, Kraft/General Foods, moved part of its coffee operations to China.[2])

Since the coffee market has fallen, first with the 1980s war and now with the recent, dramatic introduction of cheap Vietnamese Robusta beans into the world market, the *cafeteleros* (coffee barons) who once ruled El Salvador have been selling off their lands, especially in the urban central zone.[3] The country's powerful have turned to other money-making ventures, buying off former state enterprises like the phone and electric services, investing in free-trade-zone *maquila* assembly factories or turning to other rumored activities such as organized crime, especially narcotics trafficking. Much former coffee land in Santa Tecla, which abuts overcrowded San Salvador, has gone to real-estate developers who build *residenciales* like mine, designed to absorb some of the new flows of money.

The walls and guards that separate us from the cafeteleros' discarded workers and other rural migrants in their shanties in Las Margaritas are common throughout urban El Salvador, not markers of exclusive status so much as indexes of some of the highest crime rates in Latin America. Since the twelve-year war between leftist guerrillas and the U.S.-backed government ended in 1992, leaving at least 75,000 dead, "peace" has meant continued violence in El Salvador – though now categorized as "common" rather than "political."[4] (That was what the U.S. government granted me money to research there, changing narratives of violence in the postwar transition.) Las Margaritas has become a stronghold for the postwar Los Angeles-trademarked gang known as the *Mara Salvatrucha*.[5] The transformation in forms of anarchy and alarm echoes the plight of many post-conflict and post-authoritarian transitions in a globalizing era.

What was happening that day, an April day, back in 1998? My field notes (typed into the portable computer I kept wrapped in layers of plastic due to the dust) bring me back. It is unbearably hot, waves rising from asphalt, accompanied by a dizzying burr of mournful cicada-like insects. *Invierno,* the rainy season, threatened, with its promises of more heat, thundershowers, electric outages. The world somehow waiting, expecting – for what, I can't say. "And I," I write nostalgically on that strange tropical day, "am thinking about silent snowfalls, about the next midday with a slight melt and me in my cheap shoes (as always), my socks wet, trudging through the crunch-and-splash route to campus, silently grumbling to myself, hating the cold, arriving at a café, settling myself at a tiny round unbalanced table and placing my bulging backpack on the chair opposite, getting up and ordering a cappuccino, double, tall and an almond croissant, adding up to US$5.00 ..."

Five dollars for a quick double-shot of caffeine and a buttery pastry. I write those words as I think about what I have just handed to Juan, the 36-year-old man who has passed by my house saying he is collecting funds for the Fundación Remar, some sort of Christian organization for rehabilitating drug addicts and alcoholics. I have given him thirty *colones*: less than $5.00, only $3.50 in fact. I haven't held back: it is what happened to be in my wallet. "I think I gave it to him," I muse, "because he reminded me that Quakers exist. He looked sad, tired, and I have no idea if his story is true, but I want to believe it so I will." He has recounted a long story to me: I asked, and that is what anthropologists do, listen to stories, share. He said he was deported two months ago from the U.S. He said they caught him in Pigeon Park in Washington, D.C. But he also spoke of life in Wisconsin, in Minnesota, other states. Though I nodded, sympathetically I thought, he pulled some kind of Minnesota identification card out of his pocket – it looked like a social services or welfare ID card – and held it up through the barred window as if I had doubted him. "His hair thick and long in the picture, his face *asustada* [scared]," I type. "Now his hair is short. He said he had met many good Americans, that he had gone to Quaker services where people don't talk. (Now who would know this in El Salvador, who hadn't been to a service? Are there Quakers here?)" Here in El Salvador, he told me, people don't help him.

I am so grateful for that image of Quakers, believing in the communal goodness, the potential in a silent room for the truth, or something real, to arise, without prodding. (So much of fieldwork feels like prodding.) I am not Quaker, at any rate; my silent morning cappuccino ritual is as close as I'll come to such communal silence. Perhaps this is why I have handed him that money, thinking of how little it is in the U.S., less than a tall double cappuccino and almond croissant at the old Cava Java on South U in Ann Arbor, MI.

I feel good. Perhaps I have performed an act of penance – even me, the vague, doubting Presbyterian – some minimal, fleeting way to salve the conscience of a *gringa* caffeine addict. It must be that conscience that rises and sticks in my throat each day as I drive past shacks of hungry ex-coffee *cortadores* into my walled development.

But when I recount the moment to my Salvadoran partner Taylor, a man who knows poverty, he calls it stupidity. No minced words there. Stupidity. We share the house, though I pay the rent with my Fulbright dollars. I knew he would be upset with me for opening the shutters of the barred *portón* (garage-door) window to a small, scruffy man asking for money.

So many people pass by, buzz the buzzer, selling tortillas or eggs or sheets or offering gardening skills, laundry services. So many people ask for, plead for, money. Taylor demands: Why him? How could I believe some story about a charity? And then to *give* money – to *just give* money – to just give *twenty colones!* (I have lied to him. Thirty colones is more than half a day's minimum wage, and more than most of the servants, the humble *muchachas* – common even in working-class districts – earn.) At the most *two* colones, he says, exasperated. Bus fare. And to a supposed organization for drug addicts and alcoholics, he adds. You know people look at you, he says, you know people watch you, the gringa, "she must have money." Maybe if it had been a *viejito* (little old man) asking for help, maybe then, he might understand, a little.

I write in my notes: "How could I explain to him the soothing image of the Quakers? … To him, I am filled with a pathetic *lástima* (pity) for others that does not function here, except to be taken advantage of. And when someone once again *se aprovecha de mi*, he feels it too. 'What do you think he's telling his friends right now? They're laughing at the gullible gringa!' he said."

Second Encounter: Cancer and Questions

I have looked and looked for the original field notes for the second encounter. How is it I remember it so vividly? Could it be I never wrote it down, just let it play and replay, grow and metamorphose, in my head? I may have scribbled it in one of the countless little notebooks or piles of paper I carried around and sometimes misplaced before I could enter them into my computer.

It was instantly odd. It would not fit, was out of joint, jarring, and so I could not forget. The first written version I have of the encounter was composed more than two years later, after a bus carrying Taylor's older brother Arles slammed into a wall and killed him.

It is Good Friday 1998. We have joined the rest of the family: don Antonio, Taylor's father; sister Marielos and her partner Arnoldo; sister Vilma and her daughter Gaby. Lety and Arles, the oldest, have come down with their three children from Quetzaltepeque, about an hour away.

They tell me this part of Santa Tecla, in the shadow of the volcano, once formed an enormous coffee plantation called the Finca Merliot (now called Ciudad Merliot). We have gathered in a tiny, almost windowless three-room dwelling, one of hundreds of squat concrete-block rowhouses in a large, densely populated, working-class, government-funded community called the Colonia Jardines del Volcán II. Since it is a holiday, people are outside, congregating everywhere, in the front doors, on the corners. Family members wander in and out, visiting friends, running errands. I sit outside, still new and unsure of what to do or how to be helpful. Lety perches herself next to me. We watch a trio of ratty dogs trotting up the compact tree-lined pedestrian passage. We have just met an hour earlier. I look at her now: she is pretty, with cinnamon skin, loose curly black hair and large, fringed, sad brown eyes. We talk about the *alfombras*, the elaborate colored-chalk-and-sawdust designs of doves and crucifixes that the neighbors are making on the street. She isn't sure if she wants to go watch the procession, the slow, swaying ritual carrying of the crucified body of Christ through the streets.

She is tired, she says. Yes, she looks tired, I tell her. It's so hard with three little ones, I comment. She tells me it is also the *dolores*, the pain. She has cancer. Ovarian cancer. They don't have the money to pay for her medicine. She can't work. We are sitting on the narrow cracked steps that lead up to the front door, beneath a spindly lime tree. Salvadoran cicadas are buzzing in the distance, "like the horn of a pick-up truck: *chiquirun-chiquirun-ting-a-ling*," as the writer Manlio Argueta (1985: 121) describes them. Crying for the death of Christ, people say – they come out about the time of Easter, at the end of the Central American summer, to mourn, to weep. Dying with the first rain of winter. I am shocked. My mother died of ovarian cancer, a prolonged, uneasy death, ten years earlier. The event seemed to break my family apart at the time and marked my own personal emotional turmoil.

"What about social security?" I finally ask Lety, referring to the state health care that Arles must pay into as a public school teacher.

"No, they only pay for the medicine when you're in the hospital." Her mother, who spends days making and selling thick Salvadoran corn tortillas over a wood fire, helps her with the children. It is difficult to manage them all. Sometimes her mother sends out eight-year-old Lupe, the oldest girl, to deliver the tortillas. She is so tired. I tell her about my mother – quickly reassuring her that "back then" things were different. I don't mention the generous medical insurance my father's university position provided, the counseling, the surgeries and follow-up, or the then-experimental treatments of cytoxin after the conventional chemotherapy was ineffective. Without changing tone or posture Lety begins telling me about one of her brothers, how he is very good with languages and learned English quickly. He hopes to go North, she says.

I am stunned. I know that I have several bills in my wallet. I move to pull them out. But something holds me back.

Later I talk to Taylor and his sisters. *Did you know?* They have heard something vague about Lety being sick. Arles doesn't tell them much. *We should do something!* I tell them. I mean, I can help her, I can buy the medicine! They shake their heads when I announce I am ready to go to the bank, to withdraw some cash, to offer her what I can.

Vilma decides her sister-in-law is making it up, or at least exaggerating wildly, inventing dolores for pity. Not pity, Marielos interrupts: dollars. Dollars (pronounced *dólares*) for dolores. Dollars from me, the famous family gringa. "She's always complaining to us about Arles," Marielos says by way of explanation. Arles does not give her enough. Arles doesn't help. Arles isn't there. (The unsaid is that Arles has other women. Not only other women, it will later be revealed, but other children.) "What does she expect? What can we do? He's our brother." Vilma and Marielos do not frame Lety's talk of cancer as family misfortune. Rather, they see it as a ploy.

Unsure of what to do, I do not give Lety anything. My inaction haunts me. I ask about her frequently. The answer, accompanied by quizzical looks, is always the same. *I'm sure she's fine.* I do not see her again until the August *fiestas*, the holidays in celebration of San Salvador's patron saint. She looks the same.

Analysis: Complex Exchange Economies

Both of these encounters involve an exchange in which a Salvadoran offers me, an outsider – a gringa – a tiny narrative, a story of suffering. In both cases the subject of money is near or on the surface. Juan requests donations (for, or under the guise of, charity). Lety confesses her cancer and mentions medicine she cannot afford. In the first case I immediately offer up a donation, only to be censured later. In the second, I hesitate, share my own story and sympathy, perhaps hold out the hope of deferred help.

Both conversations take place in a complex grid of exchange economies. The coffee plantation setting frames our relative historical positions as bourgeois consumers of US$5.00 cappuccinos and croissants on the one hand, and generations of proletariat coffee cortadores always living at the margins on the other hand. After the fall of coffee as the main Salvadoran source of wealth during the war and the "lost decade" of the 1980s, feelings of amorphous anxiety arose in the postwar era, structured by the thickening, unbalanced flows of migrant remittances and other, sometimes mysterious, forms of capital: new investments in the ideologically free-market, neoliberal environment (though El Salvador's financial terrain is actually voraciously monopoly-capitalist), as well as suspected organized crime, and indeed the quick-grab of ubiquitous street crime. During more than three years of fieldwork between 1994 and 1999, people would often tell me, "It's worse than the war" (Moodie 2002). Though their immediate fear was rising crime, I argue such expressions also indexed an acute yet non-specific anxiety about the shadowy shifts in the economy.

The anthropologist George Marcus (1999) writes of this kind of anxiety as part of a changed mise en scène in ethnographic fieldwork, a consequence of simultaneous senses of increasing world connection (with flows of capital, people, ideas) and feelings of local disconnection from forces of change. "In any particular location," he writes, "certain practices, anxieties, and ambivalences are present as specific responses to the intimate functioning of non-local agencies and causes – for which there are no convincing common-sense understandings" (1999: 98). Marcus argues that ethnographers and their informants in this changing world seek affinity, indeed complicity, in a "mutual curiosity and anxiety [in relation] to a 'third,' ... not so much the abstract contextualizing world system but specific sites elsewhere that affect their interactions" (1999: 101).

How much are these exchanges, or attempted exchanges, that I have described linked to my identity as a conspicuous gringa (a word that always assumes a connection with the U.S. [Nelson 1999]) in the insecure postwar setting of San Salvador in the year 1998, where licit and illicit flows of dollars merge in ways still mysterious and incomprehensible? Both Juan and Lety explicitly relate to me as a North American, discussing their experience in the U.S. (in Juan's case) or their family's desires to go there (Lety). Neither Juan nor Lety initiates these exchanges with me in my role as as ethnographer and social scientist. Though I initially assumed neither interaction fell into the category in which ethics have been so carefully examined in anthropology, I realize now that the difference they both acknowledge – our unequal economic positions – is *constitutive* of anthropology. As Stefan Senders has pointed out, "Anthropologists *depend on* significant disparities of wealth and power between the knower and the known" (2004).

My partner and his family immediately characterized these quick confidences as counterfeit, as calculated (rather than sincere) moves to elicit dollars (and thus a trick rather than an exchange). But I suspect – or I want to suspect – that in each case those imagined dollars, and my pale-faced, long-nosed visage indexing them, represent a larger imagining of connection, a gesture toward complicity from which my family hopes to protect me in some way. The truth is, I believed, perhaps still believe, in some form of sincerity in both Juan and Lety. I want to imagine a humanistic, empathic connection despite all critical theory and postmodernist protest.

But I cannot help but think of the ethnographer-poet Ruth Behar's long, complicated friendship with "Esperanza," the Mexican marketing women she writes so movingly of in her monograph *Translated Woman: Crossing the Border with Esperanza's Story* (1993). It was Esperanza who sought her out, requesting financial assistance. She knocked on the door of the house Behar and her husband David Frye had rented in the dusty town of Mexquitic and asked that they enter into a *compadrazgo* relation, becoming "spiritual coparents" first for her daughter's *quinceañera* (fifteenth birthday). From the beginning, then, money framed their relationship. Behar admits she initially wondered if Esperanza saw her as "an easy source from which to tap funds" (1993: 6). Later, as Esperanza spent hours telling *historias* of her life – the life of "a battered child, battered wife, abandoned wife, unwed mother, 'Indian' marketing woman, believer in witchcraft" (Behar 1996: 153) – to Behar and a tape recorder in a green-walled room, their exchanges became more involved, tangled, complicit. At one point the marketing woman compared the anthropologist to a priest and called their sessions "confessions." For Esperanza, Behar (1996: 170) concludes, the narrative of her own life has value (and thus merits being carried to the other side – Behar's and Esperanza's "third," in Marcus' sense) because it is a narrative of the Christian soul, a story of suffering which moves from rage to redemption. Always, however, I argue (and Behar does not deny), there was money. Encounters with money.

As Behar herself (1993: 12) describes her work creating the book made out of their dialogue, she transforms their "spoken words into a commodity" and is a "peddler" of those words. These encounters with money are more than metaphors. Behar sends half her book advance to Mexico. She brings gifts – televisions, sheets – each time she visits. She sends money orders when requested. Finally, in words she later regrets, she tells Esperanza she is not sure she can continue. Esperanza immediately answers: "I won't ask for anything else, even if I'm dead and dying." She not only returns a money order, but also a copy of the book itself, recently published. "Please take this back. We don't want to be in your debt," she says (Behar 1995: 76).

Though Behar (1993: 342 and 1995: 77) suggests that in this act Esperanza refused to be the "translated woman," I would suggest that Esperanza was reacting to a deeper change in the relationship. The relationship was not corrupted by these exchanges but defined by them. Esperanza, after all, began the cycles of gifting – in the tradition of compadrazgo but also in the field of capitalist relations. One product of their exchanges is the book that at one point sits in piles of unsold inventory in Behar's mother's house.

And so it may well be that my partner, and his family, are trying to protect me (the unknowing outsider) not from two possible rip-off artists, but from the obligations of an ongoing relationship of exchange. That I may *want* those kinds of relationships, that I could see them as different kinds of opportunities (whether – to be blunt – to gather ethnographic material, emergent in our significant disparities of wealth and power, or to salve my conscience – or simply to *help* in the now-uneasy ethic of service and social justice that sent a naïve me to anthropology in the first place) does not enter their public interpretation of the interaction. (A more sympathetic reading of my partner's and family's reactions could be that they are enacting a Latin American tendency to help relatives or local community members, as opposed to a U.S. Protestant Christian notion of charity to strangers. But I wonder if some of the war-era distrust doesn't enter into this interaction as well.)

Re-encounters: Returns and Hauntings

As Taylor predicted, Juan rings our front-door buzzer again. He asks me
if I, or if my husband, might have any old clothes we could give him. I
agree to ask. I instantly regret my response. What if he returns again when
Taylor is here? The very next day he comes back (and I learn he is not
from the adjoining comunidad, Las Margaritas, as I have assumed, but
from another marginal zone a good bus ride and walk away). I tell him,
quickly, barely looking him in the eyes, that my husband does not have any
clothes (in fact I haven't asked) and it would be better if he does not come
back again. I am angry at myself and at Taylor, thinking him overly protective, even *machista*. After all, we have given clothes to many others – but
"known" others.

But even my feminist Salvadoran friends Olga and Cledys admonish me
for giving a stranger thirty colones. They both offer anecdotes about the
problems these kinds of exchanges generate. Olga, the co-owner of a prosperous industrial bakery, tells me about her German friends being the
targets of schemes. Cledys, too, a sporadically employed, poor single
mother and staunch supporter of the leftist former guerrilla party, warns
me about generosity toward strange men. She recounts the time she spon-
taneously handed two colones (about a U.S. quarter) to a Christian per-
former on a bus because he wasn't singing music degrading to women. He
then sat down next to her, talked with her, stayed on the bus until her stop,
got off with her, walked the blocks with her nearly to her house, suddenly
confessing his love for her, a stranger. She had to hide in a relative's house
until he finally gave up and left.

Unlike Juan, Lety is family. I am still haunted by our aborted Good
Friday exchange six years ago. Why does she tell me she is suffering *in her
ovaries* – her reproductive organs – in her womanhood, her motherhood?
Only later would we find out about Arles' other children (or perhaps
everyone else already knew). Though she may well have needed money –
surely *did*, they are poor – I think it is terribly significant that she expresses
herself through a description of the suffering body of a woman, to me,
another woman who will soon be structurally positioned in the family in
the same way. Perhaps, like Esperanza and Behar, she would have begun
confiding in me stories of "marriage as incarceration, as the cross and the
curse of the white wedding dress" (Behar 1996: 162).

Though I was not married to Taylor at the time, I fit into the family as
a political relative, *cuñada*, sister-in-law. Today I almost yearn for an
old-fashioned British social anthropology map of the structure of these

relations. Has her gesture toward me, her attempted exchange as a possible step toward alliance, broken some rule? Is the family's reaction, impugning Lety's integrity and telling me not to help her, an attempt to right the order of things?

In the end it will be Arles, not Lety, who dies prematurely. In November 2000 he is killed in a bus accident. His mangled body will sit alone in the morgue, unidentified, unclaimed, until the next day. Though they have separated, Lety receives a small cash settlement of about US$3,000 for his death. It turns out the bus crashed after it hit a spare tire left out in the road by a driver repairing a truck for the multinational giant Coca-Cola. The company lawyers quickly offered dollars in exchange for the victims' families' suffering.

As I revise this essay (July 2004), I am back in El Salvador, on a three-week trip dedicated to research in the national archives. This time with money from the Mellon Foundation, I am seeking discourses on criminality in the 1930s. I am taking the buses, although in our frequent phone calls Taylor, who remains in Illinois for work, keeps on warning me about specific routes and times and places. So I was thinking of cancer, and coins and charity, when a woman began to shout her story on the bus one morning. "I am seventy-nine years old," she said, or so I recall on my Macintosh a few days later. "I have had two cancerous tumors. The bottles of pills cost $35.45 each one [El Salvador dollarized in 2001]. They don't give them away. In the name of Jesus, I plead with you for a limnosa [gift] ..."

I grabbed at all the change I had in my pocket for bus fares and street beggars: about sixty cents. As I wrote that night, even the girl next to me, an adolescent with stained clothes and a small baby, handed her a nickel, as did the manicured bleached-blonde woman in a secretary uniform across the aisle (some pennies, I think). Before I knew it she was gone. I wrote in my notes,

> Now I am thinking: sixty cents? For cancer? And truly, in the moment when others were handing her nickels and pennies, it felt so generous. After all, in this country a recent discussion over raising fares by three cents raised great protest. I am watching for her now every time we pass the stop, but so far I haven't seen her again. What would I do anyway? Of course there are always others, always more people asking, pleading for help, or selling things like television antennas (this I saw today in the Plaza Barrios, so odd), wandering the streets with their wares. I swear there are more street vendors, more beggars, more children holding their hands out, more than before, maybe it really is the fall in coffee prices, or maybe it just seems so after all the time in quiet comfortable Champaign, Illinois.

Where I continue to indulge in cappuccinos.

Lety, Vilma tells me, recently lost her job at St. Jack's, a Salvadoran-owned maquila. The newspaper *La Prensa Gráfica* (July 9 2004, p. 40) reported today that maquila exports fell US$18.5 million in the first four months of 2004 in comparison to 2003. The newspaper blames "the China effect": they believe factory owners are moving to cheaper Asian countries.

Lety hasn't talked to anyone in the family (who criticize her for having "wasted" the US$3,000), but Luisito, her oldest son, told his aunt she was planning to try her luck in the U.S.

Notes

1. About 1.1 million Salvadorans living in the U.S. sent $1.92 billion in remittances to relatives in El Salvador in 2001 (data from various sources, cited in José Adán Vaquerano Amaya, "*El flujo de las remesas de los emigrantes latinoamericanos y su incidencia en las economías de la región*," *Estudios Centroamericanos* 663–4 [January–February 2004], 80). Remittances, which reached 20.9 percent of Salvadoran homes, made up 13.9 percent of the Gross National Product (GNP) in 2001 (Mario Salomón Montesino Castro, "*Economía remesera y proceso electoral*," *Estudios Centroamericanos* 665–6 (March–April 2004), 293–5).
2. Coincidentally, as I reviewed fragile yellowing newspapers in El Salvador's national archives in July 2004, I found the following entry for June 9, 1938, in the government periodical *La República* (page 4): "THE LARGEST COFFEE PROCESSOR IN THE WORLD. Hoboken, N.J. Tomorrow the construction of the largest coffee processor in the world will begin in this city, with a cost of a million dollars, covering a half-million cubic feet. There to put down the first brick of this monstrous plant will be the governor of New Jersey and the president of General Foods Corporation" (translation mine). Processors are almost always located in Europe and the United States; they heavily control market prices.
3. According to Lic. Julia del Carmen Mena, director of communications of the Salvadoran Foundation for Research on Coffee, PROCAFÉ, of El Salvador (interview with author, Santa Tecla, El Salvador, July 9, 2004), it was the massive mid-1990s arrival of Vietnam's low-quality Robusta variety beans, the product of World Bank-funded development projects, that economic analysts tie to the most recent, precipitous fall of world coffee prices. "It's the famous Asiatic effect," she said. "Cheap labor." See also Guillermo Pérez, "*Impacto económico y social de la crisis de precios bajos de café*," *Boletin Económico y Social* 210 (San Salvador: Fundación Salvadoreña para el Desarrollo Económico y Social, FUSADES, May 2003), which graphically portrays the sudden increase in production in Vietnamese product, surpassing El Salvador's area of coffee cultiva-

tion in 1995 (after negligible crops before 1988). In fourteen years the Southeast Asian country increased its plantings from 50,000 to more than 600,000 manzanas. Today Vietnam's coffee area is triple El Salvador's and far surpasses even Brazil's. Despite coffee's declining percentage of the Gross National Product (GNP), its price was actually rebounding after many owners left their crops to rot, or sold their land cheaply, during the war. In 1997, the average price per quintal of coffee rose to a height of US$154.81 (from a low of US$58.69 in 1992–3); by 2000–1, it was just US$59.14 per quintal. Thus the events in this account took place just as coffee prices were falling. In the particular case of the Santa Tecla lands, much has been sold due to rising real-estate prices, according to Mena. It is also important to remember that the coffee market fluctuates notoriously. Coffee's contribution to the GNP fell in one year from 64.2 percent in 1991 to 27.5 percent in 1992, the year the peace accords were signed. It was 19.6 percent in 2000 (statistics from *Boletín Estadístico de la Caficultura Salvadoreña Año 2001* (Nueva San Salvador: Fundación Salvadoreña para Investigaciones del Café, PROCAFÉ).

4. Statistics on violence in El Salvador have varied widely, but between 1994 and 1997 the homicide rate was reported to be more than 100 per 100,000 inhabitants per year, while in 2002 the United Nations Development Program reported a rate of 54.5 per 100,000, still among the highest in the world (Program Nacionas Unidas de Desarrollo, Informe sobre Desarrollo Humano 2003, Compendio Estadístico, 357, available in 2003 at www.desarollohumano.org).

5. During my recent research stay the newspapers and television news shows were reporting on the trial of nine gang members charged with decapitating a young university student in the comunidad Las Margaritas. The killers left her head at a bus stop and her charred body in another location. José Zometa, "*Juicio por homicidio*," *La Prensa Gráfica*, July 5 2004, 14.

CHAPTER 4

Hot Loans and Cold Cash in Saigon

Allison Truitt

By the 1990s Saigon had become a showcase for Vietnam's integration with capitalist institutions and global markets.[1] The former capital of southern Vietnam, formally renamed Ho Chi Minh City, was widely recognized as the country's center of commerce. Newly built department stores and the sudden abundance of goods for sale on street corners bespoke the promise of economic reforms. Money from foreign investment, development assistance and overseas remittances flowed into the city, but the huge influx of cash was not easily digested. People blamed the hot spots of Vietnamese society – corruption, crime and violence – on money.

If money was "hot," it could also be "cold." Cold cash was money withheld from circulation: money tucked under mattresses, stored in iron safes or buried underground. People used the phrase, "cold as cash" (*lạnh như tiền*) to describe individuals who were miserly and indifferent to the plight of others, individuals who preferred to keep money to themselves rather than offer it to others in need. I lived in Vietnam for two years with the intention of studying money and morality. What I learned instead was that I had unwittingly participated in raising the temperature of money.

Mr. Thang's Problem

It was a hot afternoon in August. I arrived home to find Mr. Hai and his teenage daughter waiting for me in the alleyway.

"How is Mr. Thang?" he asked as soon as I greeted him. I was somewhat surprised that he knew where I lived. I was even more surprised when

Mr. Hai inquired after Mr. Thang, a man in his late fifties. The two men were close friends; Mr. Thang was the one who had introduced me to Mr. Hai and his family several months before.

"Is everything all right?" I countered. Mr. Hai's daughter looked down uncomfortably at her feet. Mr. Hai was silent for a moment, and then asked me to come to his house the next day to discuss "Mr. Thang's problem."

Mr. Thang's problem was always the same. Like countless men and women in Saigon, he was chronically short of money. Of course he had some money. Pocket money. A slim stack of Vietnamese dong notes that he kept neatly folded in his front shirt pocket. A stack he always pulled out as he gallantly offered to pay for my iced coffee or the fee to park my motorbike on the sidewalk. But his display of that meager stack only confirmed what we both knew to be true: Mr. Thang was barely getting by.

In the 1990s, the Vietnamese economy posted impressive rates of growth, but the gains were not distributed evenly across society.[2] Older men and women like Mr. Thang still found money hard to come by. Those who survived did so because they had access to U.S. dollars – overseas remittances from family and friends living abroad or the petty cash of tourists. But for Mr. Thang, those dollars were just out of reach.

Mr. Thang had many stories to tell me of his friends and distant relatives who had emigrated to other countries. Like many of them, Mr. Thang had been drafted to serve in the Army of the Republic of Vietnam. After the fall of the southern Vietnamese regime in 1975, he was not sent to a re-education camp but to Hanoi, the capital of North Vietnam, where he worked on a construction site. For a few months, he felt relatively wealthy because he could afford a meal or two at a private restaurant, rather than the state-run cafeteria. When he returned to southern Vietnam, he earned a meager living as a freelance photographer. Yet when a chance came to leave the country by boat, he stayed on shore, hesitant to leave his wife and two young daughters. And in the early 1990s, his fortunes were once again overturned. The United States had instituted an asylum program for army officers who had been held in re-education camps for three or more years.[3] Mr. Thang, who had spent those years in Hanoi, was ineligible to apply. He began pedaling a cyclo, a rickshaw-bicycle used to carry passengers and market goods around the city. But he lost that job as well after his lower left leg and several fingers were amputated. His wife divorced him shortly after he left the hospital. In a city where people, goods and money were moving ever faster, Mr. Thang was reduced to riding a makeshift bicycle around the city, pedaling with his remaining leg.

Yet Mr. Thang survived. No longer able to rely on his wife, he turned to the sympathy of friends to advance him money, sometimes as loans, at other times as outright gifts. With his poverty and missing limbs reminding his friends of the sacrifices so many had made for the southern Vietnamese regime, Mr. Thang was hard to refuse, and he assumed the loans would eventually be forgiven, if not entirely forgotten.

Cold Cash in a Hot Economy

I met Mr. Thang through another friend. Mr. Thang was well-known for his level-headed advice and his deliberate views on how the city was changing. Before I met him, I was cautioned never to talk to him about money. Mr. Thang's reluctance to talk about money earned him the begrudging respect of other men in his circle whose conversations were often dominated by the topic.

The more I listened to Mr. Thang's stories, the more I realized they were also about money. The stories often turned on how he successfully avoided any discussion of money. Storytelling, he explained, was an art. One had to be sensitive to the structure of the request, to read the signs such as the mood of one's benefactor, to know the status of their relationship, and above all, to present a credible story. Credibility, I learned, was in the storyteller's ability to generate sympathy. Stories of suffering, misery and loss were currency that could be exchanged for cash.

In Vietnam, cash does more than settle debts. In the right hands, cash is a token of ongoing relatedness, and expresses intimacy, friendship and trust. Even when lending money, some people purposefully reject the appearances that would align gestures of friendship with the cold world of institutionalized exchanges. Signatures, for example, would mean the symbolic end of friendship.

As an American in southern Vietnam, I was a player in this economy of storytelling. Close friends, remote acquaintances and even strangers approached me for money. Their stories included plans to purchase wholesale goods, bus fare to visit an ailing mother, motorbike repairs, and even mobile-phone subscriptions. The fact that people made their requests in the idiom of U.S. dollars rather than Vietnamese dong indicated the strange and magical place of foreign currency in Vietnam's rapidly expanding economy. Like a long-term loan from the Asian Development Bank, the money I lent was not quite charity, but rarely, if ever, repaid.

When Mr. Thang approached me for money the first time, he did so cautiously, explaining that he needed a hundred dollars to purchase material for school uniforms and pay tuition for his two daughters in high school. At the end of his story, he punctuated his story with a "what do you think of that," as if he did not quite believe it himself. The image of his school-age daughters caught me off-guard. I quickly convinced myself that I was learning something from him and could – perhaps even should – pay him for our conversations as I had paid others for more formal language instruction. So I became complicit in the economy of intimacy in which stories could be exchanged for cash, but without ever outright acknowledging what we each thought the money represented.

Mr. Thang's "problem" had become even more urgent by autumn. To my surprise, he introduced me to his new wife, a young woman in her early twenties who was simply called *út*, or "the little one." She had moved to the city to sell coffee and bottles of beer on a street corner. Her boss was a distant relative. Mr. Thang frequently stopped by her stand, and after a few months he suggested, against the advice of his friends, that they move in together. His friends were dismayed that he had set up a household with such a young woman, convinced that she had moved because she thought Mr. Thang had money. A young woman from the countryside, they warned, had too many expectations for what a husband from the city could provide, especially one who was an amputee. But Mr. Thang felt confident that he and his young wife would get by in Saigon's buoyant economy.

They rented a small room facing a dusty street in District Seven in a neighborhood that was several bridges away from the center of the city. From their street-front residence, they planned to sell coffee and other sundries to residents in the neighborhood, or so Mr. Thang assured me. The rented room had the appearance of a shop. A glass case was stocked with an odd assortment of shampoos and soaps, batteries and other gadgets that he hoped to sell. And along the back wall of their rented room was his unsold inventory of postcards, old stamps and ceramic knick-knacks. Whenever I visited, his wife would quickly brew a cup of coffee for me, and Mr. Thang would hastily set up a few plastic folding chairs. He never accepted money for the coffee he served me, and I was not sure whether he actually sold any coffee at all. On one occasion, his landlady came over and asked for "half a cup," but he refused to accept money from her.

More often, Mr. Thang came to my neighborhood, but he never came directly to my door. He instead asked Mrs. Tinh, a woman who sold beverages to residents in the alleyway, to fetch me. "You've got a visitor waiting," she would say, "the man with one leg." He waited at one of the small plastic tables that Mrs. Tinh had lined up along the wall. Each time he inquired about my research and then described his own plans to set up a noodle shop or sell souvenirs in the center of the city ... if only he had the cash to do so.

I was first drawn in by Mr. Thang's stories. But over the months I learned that as a foreigner, debts to me were not quite loans, but something else: a transfer of wealth, restitution for past wrongs or a sudden windfall. At first I accepted people's requests as an informal price for conducting fieldwork in Vietnam, but I gradually reconciled my position as a fieldworker who accumulated inevitable and often immeasurable debts with a more sensible approach. I learned how to ward off such requests, gently but firmly, with stories of my own.

Mr. Thang was persistent. His most phenomenal story was that his young wife was pregnant. I eventually agreed to advance him some money to jumpstart a trade so he would be able to provide for his family. On the day we agreed to meet, he instead asked me to accompany him to the hospital. His wife had delivered a stillborn. When I entered the crowded hospital room, I saw her lying on a hospital bed, clasping her worn handbag close to her chest, surrounded by women holding their newborns. Mr. Thang remarked bitterly as I handed him the cash, the seed money for a small business, that he had to pay the hospital bill whether the baby was born dead or alive. "This couldn't all be staged, could it?" I wondered in disbelief as I stood at the foot of the bed where his young wife lay.

When Mr. Hai approached me on that August afternoon to discuss "Mr. Thang's problem," I was annoyed. Had Mr. Thang finally recruited Mr. Hai to make a plea for money on his own behalf? Still, I agreed to go to his house that day.

The Deal

It was Mr. Thang who had introduced me to Mr. Hai. He explained that his ex-wife was distantly related to Mr. Hai's wife's first husband. Their friendship endured in spite of the criss-crossed lines of kinship. Mr. Hai's family earned a living by selling pork from a small two-room house in District Four. The neighborhood, just a few blocks from the Saigon port, was widely regarded by many people in the city as a place of danger and crime. But the neighborhood was no different than so many other neighborhoods in the city. People pushed carts of street food up and down the narrow alleys. Houses were quickly built up with second and third floor additions, their ground-floors raised and tiled. In the large square, the concrete building that housed the indoor market could not contain all the buying and selling. Traders spilled into the streets surrounding the market – baskets of fruit and vegetables, piles of clothes and tarps laden with fish and pieces of meat were lined up around the market square and filled the side streets. In the early morning hours, the tightly packed crowds of vendors and shoppers made it impossible to move through the narrow streets by motorbike or even bicycle. Here commerce, if not transparent, was certainly visible.

The next afternoon, I arrived at Mr. Hai's house. He was sitting with several of his friends on the cement floor of his house. They clustered around a small charcoal burner, grilling pork and pouring each other cheap rice wine from a plastic bottle. "Drinking and eating," or *nhậu*, as it is popularly called in southern Vietnam, is associated with idle consumption. As the men grilled their pork and poured round after round of the rice wine, they also bantered about city politics, gossiped about their acquaintances and stuck deals, all over that small charcoal burner.

Mr. Hai called to his son to bring me a glass of iced coffee. He then took out a piece of paper, his face slightly flushed from the wine. On the top of the paper was written, "10,000,000 dong" (about US$640 in 2001), followed by a list of months – May, June, July and September – each followed by the sum, "1,000,000 dong." The significance of that piece of paper, so obvious to all the men in the room, meant nothing to me. Sensing my bewilderment, Mr. Hai then recounted the terms of the deal. He had loaned Mr. Thang ten-million dong with the promise that I, his American friend, would send Mr. Thang US$300 over the summer and then give him a used motorbike to sell for cash in September. Mr. Thang had paid 1,000,000 dong in the months of May and June, but had then disappeared. It was now the end of August, and Mr. Hai wanted the rest of the money.

I was dumbfounded. While I knew Mr. Thang's problem would eventually arrive at money, I never expected that I would be implicated in a loan between these two men. I had arrived expecting to refuse a request rather than deny my involvement.

"Isn't this all true?!" he exploded.

I quickly tried to calculate what I had just heard: 10 million dong, 1 million dong, 300 U.S. dollars and one motorbike. How did it all add up? It was true that Mr. Thang was the registered owner of the motorbike I used. As a foreigner, I was not permitted to own registered property. But in Saigon, ownership and possession rarely coincide. Motorbikes, like money, are the very means of mobility in the city. They are among the most easily bought and sold assets that people possess. Consequently, most people do not even trouble themselves to change the registration of a second-hand motorbike. Mr. Thang did so only at my request, leading us both on a bureaucratic adventure that consumed three entire days. That made the motorbike legally his. But why then did Mr. Thang claim I promised him US$300? I stammered in reply to Mr. Hai that I had never made such promises and then countered with my own story:

"Why, how could I have promised him my motorbike when I needed to sell it to have enough money to buy an airline ticket back to the U.S.?"

Mr. Hai then slammed his hand on the wooden platform bed as he prodded his friends to verify his recollections of that day.

"He sat right there," Mr. Hai shouted. "He drank with us, he ate with us, he agreed to the terms."

He then quickly pinned blame, neither on Mr. Thang nor on me, but on Mr. Thang's young wife.

"This never happened before he got married," he said, as he shook his head.

It was an old but familiar story. A man, once trustworthy and true to his word, was corrupted by a woman's insatiable material desires. He then pointed to his motorbike, warning that he would have to sell his own motorbike, leaving his children stranded with no transportation to school. He stood up and pushed me out the door with a perfunctory invitation to come by should I ever need help. I found myself back on the narrow street, now deserted after the day's buying and selling had come to an end. Mr. Hai's wife asked me to come in. I stammered an apology, "Mr. Thang ... I didn't know ... I'm sorry," and then left.

Hot Loans

I looked down at the piece of paper in my hands, still confused by the turn of events and my own unwitting role in the deal. How was I to know that Mr. Thang had made such promises that I would give him a few hundred dollars and my motorbike? The piece of paper listed only numbers and months. Surely this piece of paper had no legal standing – it was not even signed. All the same, it signaled an agreement of some sort between the two men. And the fact that the piece of paper was now in my hand was evidence of my own complicity.

I then took the piece of a paper to an acquaintance and gave him a brief summary of my conversation with Mr. Hai. I explained that one man had loaned another a sum of money based on the promise that I would give the borrower my motorbike and cash. He then burst out laughing at my account. This was not a case of money exchanging hands between friends as I had imagined, but a "hot loan" (*vay nóng*). He suspected Mr. Thang had agreed to pay 1 million dong every month, not towards the balance of the loan, but as a "fee" for using the money until he could repay the 10 million dong in full. "But these two men are friends," I insisted. He shrugged as if that made no difference. I asked others, and everyone I consulted for an alternate interpretation nodded knowingly, "hot loan."

I had read about hot loans. The state-run press reported widely on these loans that carry steep interest rates by the month, week or even day. Hot loans are not governed by impersonal institutions. They are deals struck between individuals, guaranteed by one's word, and backed by the threat of violent retribution should the terms of repayment not be met. In the state-run press, these moneylenders were depicted as eager profiteers who conduct furtive agreements in alleyways.

Hot loans, however, were a necessary response to the otherwise undeveloped credit markets in Vietnam. The state-run banking sector offered credit primarily to large companies owned by the central government and its various branches. Obtaining credit for would-be entrepreneurs was a chronic problem. Individuals who could not draw on the resources of friends and family had to find other means of raising cash in the face of the numerous restrictions imposed by the state. Hot loans, pawnshops and small associations of acquaintances or colleagues provided people with cash quickly, but often on terms that could not be met.

Was Mr. Thang's problem then anything more than a hot loan? Did Mr. Hai agree to lend the money merely on the promise that an American and her forthcoming dollars would fulfill the terms of the deal? How did Mr. Thang imagine the deal would play out? Or was "Mr. Thang's problem" just an elaborate scheme in which I had been caught? I shuddered as I recalled that my failure to see that deal between the two men as a hot loan had protected me from Mr. Hai. I had not seen Mr. Hai as a money-lender, but as a friend of Mr. Thang who had introduced me as an ongoing gesture of friendship ... not as a set-up. And I had believed that Mr. Hai had advanced the money to Mr. Thang, not as a usurious loan, but as a way to help out an old friend. But Mr. Hai neither knew nor cared why Mr. Thang had needed ten million dong so urgently. When I asked him that afternoon, he merely shrugged and rambled off a few reasons: Mr. Thang needed the money to fix up his house, or to send to his wife's family in the countryside, or even to purchase a bigger television set.

It was months before Mr. Thang appeared again in the alleyway where I lived. He showed no remorse over how he had converted his friendship with me into ten million dong. He admitted matter-of-factly that Mr. Hai was well-known for making hot loans, and he had attempted to do the same. A few months earlier, he had been approached for a loan by a brother and sister who sold pork in front of his rented room in District Seven. He borrowed the ten million dong from Mr. Hai who only needed the assurance that his American friend would make good on the loan. Mr. Thang, in turn, was sure that the brother and sister would do a good business because he had watched how much pork they sold everyday. But within a few days, they disappeared along with the money. He then heard rumors that the man had needed money to repay gambling debts. Mr. Thang struggled for several months to meet the terms of his agreement with Mr. Hai, but after a few months he could no longer keep up. He and his wife then disappeared into one of the many alleyways in their neighborhood, forsaking a potentially lucrative street-front property for a secluded residence where Mr. Hai could not find them. Only a few close friends knew where they lived. Mr. Thang no longer dropped by the café where he had been a regular for twenty years. He even stopped attending a Sunday church service out of fear that Mr. Hai might be waiting for him across the street. But he still insisted that Mr. Hai would never kill him: "As long as I'm alive, there is the chance that I will repay him." What I had once understood to be the warm relations of mutual obligations and reciprocity had cooled down considerably. He invited me to visit the small garage that he rented only a few blocks from where Mr. Hai lived. I did so once. And when I returned to Saigon in 2003, I found that Mr. Thang was still there.

His workshop was little more than a concrete slab. He sat on the floor while he repaired fans, rice cookers and cassette players. On the concrete floor were scattered nuts and bolts, and his clothes were even more tattered than the last time I had seen him. A piece of duct tape held the strained fabric of his pants together in several places. When he saw me he grinned and announced he had some unexpectedly good news.

He pointed to an old Honda motorbike parked on the street. A friend had given him the bike, which he had refashioned to use with his amputated leg. His wife was thrilled that they would now be able to ride around the city on Saturday nights. But I could hardly believe what he told me next. His landlady's sister-in-law, now an American citizen, was arranging for him to emigrate to the U.S. His landlady had been married to a high-ranking officer in the South Vietnam army. Her husband's entire family had sought asylum in the U.S. When the family returned, the sister-in-law declared it disgraceful that a veteran of the Republic of Vietnam Army should live in such abject poverty. She vowed to help Mr. Thang and his wife to move to the U.S. and then to provide them with housing and employment.

Over the years I had known Mr. Thang, he had described the U.S. as a place where he could be made whole again. Mr. Thang's own life fortunes had waxed and waned in relationship to his proximity to the U.S. As a military recruit in the South Vietnam army, he had been paid a reliable salary. But as a former soldier for the defeated south, he barely eked out a living in the street. His skills in repairing electrical appliances were nothing special. On this one street alone, he pointed out, four or five people also repaired small appliances. But in the U.S. his body would be healed with a prosthetic limb and his labor fairly compensated.

Money in Saigon's tumultuous circuits of exchange followed drastic cycles in which fortunes could be made or squandered overnight as borrowers became lenders, and lenders were sold on a story. The vast infusion of money into Vietnam's economy altered the parameters of friendship and finance. My relationship with Mr. Thang was thoroughly structured by money even though I pretended otherwise. Mr. Thang had successfully converted his friendship with me into collateral for a hot loan, transforming the warmth of gifted money into the heat of borrowed money. Ironically, his success in obtaining the loan demonstrated that Mr. Hai believed Mr. Thang just as much as I did. In the end, the warmth of friendship had cooled considerably in Saigon's overheated economy. Mr. Hai lost money, Mr. Thang abandoned his home, and I was left holding a piece of paper.

Notes

1. The slogan for the officially sanctioned market-oriented reforms of the Vietnamese economy initiated in 1986 is Đổi Mới or "Renovation." Some scholars argue that economic liberalization in Vietnam was not the deliberate outcome of policies, but rather informal processes (see Fforde and de Vlyder 1996).

2. Economic growth averaged 8 percent annually between 1990 and 1997. While Vietnam maintained positive income growth during the Asian Financial crisis,

foreign direct investment declined and the Vietnamese state took a more direct role in stimulating growth (Luong 2003).

3. The Orderly Departure Program was a legal alternative for qualified applicants to emigrate to the U.S. In 1989, a special ODP subprogram processed former re-education camp detainees and their immediate family members.

CHAPTER 5

The Smoking Wallet

An Anthropologist Meets Transnational Tobacco Corporations in Malawi

Marty Otañez

This chapter grew out of a question I asked myself while I was in Malawi, where I was doing research on tobacco workers' unions. During my stay, I gave some money to a union leader whose help had been important to my research, and with whom I had become friendly – I'll call him Eugene.[1]

At the same time, a foundation sponsored by a consortium of tobacco companies offered Eugene money, too. They paid him to administer a "corporate social-responsibility" project – a project meant to draw attention away from the tobacco companies' unfair labor practices.

Eugene was happy to accept the money I offered him. He was also happy to accept the money the tobacco company foundation offered him. I was working to expose the practices of tobacco corporations in Malawi, and I saw the money I gave Eugene as a way toward that goal. The tobacco companies were working to burnish their image, and they saw the money they gave Eugene as a way toward that goal. I worried about this. Wasn't I trying to burnish my image, too? Wasn't I doing the same thing the tobacco companies were? I felt there was a difference. More importantly, I wanted Eugene to feel there was a difference. But I'm not sure he did. In retrospect, I'm not sure it was possible.

I made five trips to Malawi between 1997 and 2003 – a total of sixteen months of fieldwork – to collect ethnographic data on the tobacco farm workforce and the tobacco industry.[2] Tobacco workers in Malawi earn an average of US$80 for a nine-month growing season – if they are paid. Many tobacco workers never receive payment for their work. They remain indebted, or bonded, to a tobacco landlord who docks their wages for fertilizers, seeds and food, often at inflated prices. Black Malawians owned all of the farms where I conducted my research. Virtually all of them were absentee landlords.

In Malawi, Philip Morris and other tobacco companies purchase tobacco from local subsidiaries of U.S.-based leaf merchants. Two of these, Universal and Alliance One International, buy virtually all of Malawi's crop. Leaf merchants routinely engage in price-fixing on local auction floors where tobacco is sold to global buyers.[3] Over 95 percent of Malawi's crop is exported. No manufactured cigarettes are produced in Malawi. Philip Morris and its colleagues profit from that price-fixing, and from tobacco whose low prices both derive from, and perpetuate, poverty, labor exploitation and deforestation in Malawi.

Altria, Philip Morris' parent company, posted net revenues of over US$89 billion in 2004. But growing public awareness that tobacco and tobacco-related products kill 5,000,000 people each year has damaged the reputations both of Philip Morris and of the world's other transnational tobacco companies. One way these companies have fought damage to their public image is by funding "corporate social-responsibility" projects. Tobacco companies use these projects to enhance their reputations, and to conceal the ways in which they and their agents abuse labor practices and monopolize buying practices. They fund school construction, HIV/AIDS orphans programs, and other poverty-alleviation activities, but they still won't pay a living wage to adult farm workers, or pay fair prices for tobacco.

One "corporate social-responsibility" project is a non-profit organization in Geneva called ECLT – Eliminating Child Labor in Tobacco-Growing. An alliance of tobacco corporations, tobacco workers' unions and tobacco growers, ECLT's stated goal is to produce research about child labor used in tobacco-growing, to support and fund projects, and to disseminate ideas about best practices in the tobacco-growing industry. ECLT budgeted a total of US$2 million for its pilot project in Malawi from 2003 to 2006.

In Malawi, this organization, in turn, paid Eugene, a key labor leader in the tobacco workers' union (the Tobacco Tenants and Allied Workers' Union) to administer a school construction project. The project site happened to be in the area where I conducted my ethnographic fieldwork. And Eugene was a key informant and a friend of mine.

I had already solved some of the doubts I had about fieldwork by situating myself as an anthropologist who was also a political activist. The Ph.D. I was working for would allow me greater access to arenas in which I could expose the practices of transnational tobacco corporations.

Yet my own ethical views made little difference once I was in Malawi. I wielded a lot less influence than the global tobacco industry. Yet Philip Morris and I shared a business strategy. We were both able to pay Malawians to further our projects, and we did so. Philip Morris and other tobacco firms, through the ECLT, paid Eugene to administer a school construction project. I gave Eugene US$600 for motorcycle repairs, fuel expenses and printing costs for trade-union membership cards.

Komana or a "Chance Encounter" with a Tobacco Company Executive

During one of my visits, I was able to videotape interviews with tobacco workers and industry executives for a film report for the Television Trust for the Environment (UK) that aired on BBC World Television in the fall of 2003. The episode, entitled "Up in Smoke," reported on Malawi's extreme dependence on tobacco cultivation. My film's prospective broadcast on BBC World Television added luster to my research, and provided me with a rare opportunity to interview and accompany a Philip Morris executive on a visit to a tobacco industry corporate social responsibility project in Malawi. A Philip Morris USA vice-president – Nick Thomsen – invited me on a day-long tour of tobacco industry-funded social responsibility project sites in Malawi. An official from ECLT had told Thomsen about my film project. Due to the history of secrecy of U.S. cigarette manufacturers, I probably could not have met such an important figure on my own.

One Saturday morning in March 2003, Nick Thomsen, the ECLT official who had introduced the two of us and I departed in a Land Rover on a tour of project sites 100 kilometers north of Lilongwe, Malawi's capital city. I told Thomsen what I was doing. He asked that our conversation remain off the record. I agreed, thinking to myself that our encounter represented a watershed moment in my fieldwork. It was the first chance I had had to meet a Philip Morris executive. It would be the first time I had been able to view a tobacco industry-funded project site.

We raced on paved and dirt roads to Dowa District in a caravan with another Land Rover carrying executive members of Total LandCare Management. Total LandCare was a reforestation project in Malawi run in partnership with Washington State University at Pullman. I knew Philip Morris had paid them US$600,000 over five years. In Dowa, we were shown a variety of tobacco industry-funded activities. Tobacco workers and farmers showed us tree seedlings, shallow wells, treadle pumps and school construction projects. Thomsen made a speech to around thirty men and women. It was translated into Chinyanja, the local language. "In order for me to help you," Thomsen told the villagers, "we need to help each other."

Listening to the Philip Morris executive speak this way to the tobacco workers and farmers that generated its wealth outraged me. I had said things like that to tobacco workers and farmers during my interviews. But Philip Morris was using its money and its programs for public relations purposes. I knew I would continue to oppose the company's practices when I went home. But compared to Philip Morris – and to me – the typical Malawian had barely enough money for basic needs. After my *komana* ("chance encounter" in Chinyanja) with Thomsen, I began to think about how money changed social interactions between labor union workers and anthropologists.

Cash Inducements and Other Interventions in Local Labor Politics

During my fieldwork in Malawi, I got to know the labor organizers of the tobacco workers' union in Nkhotakota, the site of the union headquarters. They took me to fourteen tobacco farms. I interviewed over eighty men and women who had spent their lives growing, harvesting and processing tobacco. I talked to them for around an hour apiece. In some cases, I conducted multiple interviews with the same person. I wanted to document abusive labor practices, such as debt servitude to local landlords who produce the majority of Malawi's burley tobacco. I wanted to understand the way labor activists recruited members, trained them and organized protests. It was during my first research trip for this project in 1997 that I met Eugene.

Eugene was one of the union's lead organizers. He had helped start the tobacco workers' union. The secretary general of the Malawi Congress of Trade Unions gave me Eugene's name. When he wasn't working with the tobacco workers' union, Eugene sang in his church choir. He belonged to a lot of church committees, committees that worked on finance, outreach and education.

Eugene invited me to union meetings on remote tobacco farms. I got to go to union meetings, and to meet unionists and farm workers. I interviewed workers about what they did every day, and what their relations with the men who ran the farms were like. In each of my five research visits to Malawi, Eugene and I got closer and closer. We went to church gatherings. He invited me to his home to eat, and to other social occasions. Eugene was indispensable in my fieldwork – it would have been virtually impossible for me to understand labor conditions in Malawi without him. I would never have been able to go to tobacco farms or to meet farm workers without his introductions.

While I was in Malawi, Eugene was put in charge of a tobacco company project. The same things that made Eugene an indispensable contact for me also made him an attractive candidate to the ECLT officials.

Eugene was now one of my research informants, and a project administrator paid by the same tobacco industry whose exploitative labor practices were at the core of my research. The union's organizing plan required Eugene to regularly visit farms and conduct branch meetings in remote areas of Malawi. Eugene allowed me to accompany him. He rode a motorcycle. He sometimes had to bring other union leaders to branch meetings, and, when he did, he took them on the back of his motorcycle. When I wanted to go, too, I caused them trouble. There were times when Eugene would shuttle me and another union leader up to forty kilometers from the main road to farms, and back again. Organizers who would normally ride with Eugene were asked to use *matola* (public transportation – a minibus, for example) while Eugene took me on his motorcycle directly to tobacco farms. In these situations, I paid for the person's matola ride. In other instances, organizers who depended on rides from Eugene decided to miss the meeting so I could ride along with Eugene.

To show my appreciation for Eugene's role in the study, I compensated him in multiple ways. I filled up his motorbike's gas tank before or after farm visits. I purchased spare parts for his motorcycle, paid for motorcycle repairs, and covered the annual license and registration fees for his motorcycle for one year. During my visits to Malawi, I gave his children football jerseys, blankets and toy action heroes, and I bought his wife beauty supplies. I purchased paper stock for union membership cards. I probably spent a total of about US$600 on all of these things. I understood them as a way for an "affluent" Westerner to show my appreciation for Eugene's role in my study.

I funded my longest fieldwork visit to Malawi in 2000 through student loans. I budgeted US$450 per month for eight months. This is a lot of money in Malawi, where the average per capita income each month is US$15. (By contrast, my budget was quite low compared to other scholars at my level in the field, who are given about US$2,500 per month by the Fulbright Program, the Wenner-Gren Foundation or the Social Science Research Council, three mainstream sources that fund graduate students conducting anthropological fieldwork.) Ideally, I would have paid Eugene US$30 per day as a research assistant. I could have given him the food and living allowances, or the US$3,000 for 100 days of fieldwork assistance, set out in the standards of the University of Malawi. I was unable to pay Eugene this much as I was simply unable to afford it.

Membership Cards: Anthropological Research as Political Work

The shortage of membership cards was a key problem for tobacco workers' union organizers. Union leaders give workers membership cards. They certify that the worker participates in the union. When a work-related problem occurs on a farm, and members ask branch leaders to come and help them, farm landlords or managers make the branch leaders show their cards before they can enter the farm. Typically, if the organizer can't show a card, landlords won't let them in. Landlords or managers would say that they did this to protect their farms and their workers, but workers and trade unionists in Malawi told me that this was really a way to obstruct union organizing. When the union was established in 1997, Eugene and his fellow organizers gave out membership cards that they had arranged to have printed on heavy colored paper stock. He said they felt that using heavy paper stock rather than lightweight stock symbolized the union's status as a permanent and bona-fide organization with the authority to represent workers' interests. Eugene told me that the year before I had come, they had run out of card stock. The new ones were printed on scraps of recycled white paper.

Union membership cards meant more than just union membership. Mona, a 25-year-old tobacco worker I interviewed, revealed to me the social value of union cards. After joining the tobacco workers' union at a meeting in Nkhotakota in September 1999, Mona received a membership card. She was happy, since the card would provide her with a form of identification that could be used in case she died on the way home at the end of the tobacco season. Workers were being found dead along the road more and more often in Malawi. They were succumbing to overwork, starvation and HIV/AIDS – all the result of the poverty with which they struggled. They couldn't pay for transportation home. Now, if Mona died on the way home, her identity card would give her home address to the people who found her. She would be given a funeral service with many people in attendance, and a marked grave near her ancestors.

I talked to many tobacco workers and labor activists about funerals. At the time I was in Malawi, labor disputes over funerals were becoming more common. Landlords were burying workers on their farms instead of sending them back to their home villages. Several of the men and women I interviewed talked about how important it was to have many people come to a funeral, and how important it was to be buried near one's ancestors, in one's home village. If Mona were found dead, and put in an unmarked grave far from her home village, her spirit would remain unsettled. It might disturb the living.

A membership card for a tobacco worker was a tangible benefit of joining the union. And the card, which held its member's name, home address, and union name and address, made tobacco workers feel safer.[4]

Without extra money or the proper personal contacts, tobacco workers in Malawi had little or no access to identity cards. The union was one of the only places they could get a card. Receiving a card was one of the things that added appeal to union membership. Membership cards connected farm workers to events and institutions at national and global levels. Organizers came to meetings and talked about union victories and alliances with groups like the United Nations' International Labor Organization.

Membership cards helped organizers, too. In order to get a card, workers had to pay monthly membership fees, and to promise to maintain employment status as a tenant or seasonal laborer in the tobacco sector. But the organizers had difficulty collecting union dues because workers were rarely paid in cash. Workers often left their farms. When they left the union, the union lost funding. The union received aid from an assortment of foreign sources, including the Catholic Church in Ireland and the national trade union movement in Norway. They couldn't get these funds without proving that their membership was growing.

Money given to the tobacco workers, Eugene told me, should "come from the heart." I decided to give Eugene the money to print union cards. I gave him US$150, a sum equivalent to the annual salaries of two tobacco workers. It paid for 2,500 union cards.

Eugene wanted to use the cards to recruit new members and strengthen the union. Several months before we actually bought the cards, Eugene and I talked about their design and content, sharing different ideas about the size and color of the tobacco leaf that stood prominently on the front of membership cards. Above all, the card had to be easy for members to carry.

Eugene and I agreed to investigate prices for printing cards separately. This allowed me to get an idea of printing costs. I worried that Eugene would get the money from me to print cards, use a "friend" to print the cards at half the quality and cost, and keep the rest of the money. I knew how money worked in Africa. As a graduate student ten years earlier, I had lived and studied in Nigeria for sixteen months, and I had now spent a significant amount of time in Malawi. In both countries I had experienced bribery, extortion and all kinds of other nefarious money practices. People were forever asking for money. This was what made me suspicious of Eugene.

Eugene had the cards printed in the fall of 2000 with the money I gave him, and he gave me two membership cards. He explained that union organizers distributed the cards to members. When I went back a year later, I wasn't surprised when Eugene told me that the cards had run out, and asked me for more money. Once I had brought money into the relationship, we fell into the pattern common to relations between Westerners and non-Westerners. Everybody asked me for money. Close friends from Malawi asked me for money. Strangers on the street asked me for money. I told Eugene that I could not give him the money. I had said no to Eugene before. He had asked me for a thousand dollars to pay for tuition for some of his children at a private school. (When I refused him that time, his words about giving "from the heart" rang in my ears.) He had asked me for a computer for the union. Labor leaders close to Eugene had asked me to buy a vehicle for the union.

Now Eugene was asking for money for more cards. Refusing to give money to so many farm workers was relatively easy, especially since I had what I thought was relatively little money to do research in Malawi. I told him I could not give him the money. My refusals of Eugene's request for money by telling him I was financially unable (which I thought to be true) were some of the most unsettling episodes of my fieldwork. I had a plan for doing "ethical" anthropology. I was going to help tobacco workers once I returned to the U.S. Or, at the very least, I was going to spread my resources across a group of workers, not just aid a single family. Eugene didn't see it that way.

To Eugene, I was a relatively wealthy Westerner with expensive audio and video equipment, and money to enhance my authority as a foreign researcher. I enjoyed the luxury of being able to leave the U.S. six times to study the lives of workers in Malawi. By giving money to Eugene, I had revealed myself as an agent of an assortment of values looping through capitalist individualism, the protection of human rights, corporate accountability and a moral discourse of reciprocity (referred to as Western "modernity") in less developed societies.

Eugene could have responded by refusing to take me to tobacco farms thereby virtually ending my fieldwork, but he didn't. He showed me that he was disappointed with frowns and other non-verbal forms of communication. This was typical. Most Malawians show respect and deference in their interactions with foreigners. We were still close. Nothing changed. But Eugene's requests and my refusals made the power imbalance in our interactions clear.

As an activist, Eugene was faced every day with organizational and legal obstacles that were rooted in poverty. He was a citizen of a country with little or no power, in a global economy dominated by U.S. capital. I hoped that my relationship with Eugene was more human than the fly-by-night encounters of tobacco company executives like Nick Thomsen. I hoped I was an exception to the example of impersonal and infrequent encounters that non-Westerners experienced at the hands of Westerners in Malawi and other non-dominant societies. But I wasn't sure. In a sense, the money I gave Eugene might have done no more than tip the imbalance in our relations farther toward dependence.

By purchasing membership cards for the union and providing other inducements to Eugene, I hoped to demonstrate publicly and financially my support for labor struggles in Malawi. By doing so, I won trust from human rights activists, union members and tobacco workers. I hoped that the access I secured led to research that would bring tobacco workers' concerns in Malawi to the attention of more people.

After I returned to the U.S., I worked to tell audiences about the social cost of tobacco through the case study of Malawi. The research generated discussion on ways to publicly oppose the industry's profiting from abusive labor conditions in Malawi and other developing societies. Between February 2002 and September 2005, I spoke and previewed my films on tobacco workers in Malawi at universities, professional academic organizations, religious groups, film festivals and other grassroots organizations in and outside California.[5]

Taking Apart Money Relationships

There was another complication in my relationship with Eugene. This
dilemma came from my conviction that Eugene's ability to represent
workers' interests might be compromised by being on the tobacco industry
payroll. I told him I disapproved of the union's decision to cooperate with
tobacco companies on child labor projects. Things got tense between us
when Eugene agreed to receive payments for his work as a local administrator for the Eliminating Child Labor in Tobacco-Growing project.[6] As it
turned out, my values of labor rights and corporate accountability con-
flicted with Eugene's. He valued labor rights, but he also valued corporate
solidarity.

Meanwhile, I was trying to analyze and disseminate examples of labor
exploitation to build political momentum against the role of tobacco companies in Malawi. I argued that union-industry collaborations were a lot
better for the tobacco industry than they were for local unions. I told
Eugene that collaborating helped tobacco firms increase their legitimacy,
and contributed to myths that tobacco production promoted economic
development and gave workers decent jobs. Using the tobacco workers'
union in child labor-free projects just increased the economic and political
leverage of the global tobacco industry in Malawi. I speculated that Philip
Morris would soon broadcast public service announcements on U.S. television featuring African children in schools built by Philip Morris, and
boasting about the firm's efforts to address the child labor problem in
Malawi. Union-industry alliances also provide global firms with opportunities to further deflect attention away from harmful monopolistic buying
practices and their aggressive marketing campaigns to hook women and
children in Malawi on cigarettes.

On numerous occasions I asked Eugene for his views on union-industry
alliances, and about projects run by tobacco companies in Malawi. We
talked about it one day at the site of an industry-sponsored school construction project that stood in the center of the industry's efforts to appear
socially responsible. He said that children on nearby tobacco farms and in
villages would obtain an education from the school. He didn't show any
sign of harboring internal conflicts about the fact that tobacco industry
money had funded the school. He did say that the Association to
Eliminate Child Labor in Malawi, an organization funded by the tobacco
industry through the ECLT, was "a tool for protecting the tobacco companies," and was comprised of people who were more interested in protecting the reputation of global tobacco companies than eliminating child

labor. He did understand that global tobacco companies used these projects in public relations efforts to present themselves as responsible institutions.

But Eugene's view of the tobacco companies was more complex. On the one hand, he suggested that tobacco companies used social-responsibility projects to promote their social and economic interests. On the other hand, he suggested that the companies should more fully involve the union in their social-responsibility projects. It was too simple to say that Eugene had been corrupted by his involvement with big tobacco companies, or that he was merely acting strategically, or that he was doing both. His remarks confirm the strength of the "stakeholder partnerships" rhetoric that tobacco companies have been using so successfully through the ECLT; they also confirm the shifting power relations in Malawi's tobacco sector. Eugene said, "We need to work together – the employer, the worker, the government, and even those [industry-funded] non-governmental organizations. I think we can fight child labor. If each one of us is opting to work on its own, then I'm afraid child labor cannot end."

Eugene chose simultaneously to align himself both with an anthropologist who wanted to make tobacco companies accountable, and with a tobacco company interested in cheap labor costs, inexpensive tobacco prices and high corporate profits. Cash disbursements from anthropologists did not keep him from taking money and other resources from corporate elites.

I viewed tobacco companies as one of the primary sources of Malawi's extreme reliance on tobacco and dependence on child labor. Eugene saw them as influential players in the trade union movement, and in the local political economy of tobacco.

While my awareness of the moral-economic conundrum grew, and my interests turned to the obstacles to effective tobacco control measures in Malawi and the impact of these measures on tobacco workers, I re-examined the relationship of trust between Eugene and other collaborators and myself. My commitment and loyalty to labor activists and workers' struggles were encoded in my repeated interactions with them and in my willingness to give money to labor advocates. Now, as I returned to the United States, I had a new worry: Was I betraying my collaborators by revealing Philip Morris' harmful business practices in Malawi?

If I worked with tobacco control groups and corporate accountability campaigners to compel Philip Morris and other tobacco companies to put public health above corporate profits, then I was undermining the industry the tobacco workers' union needed in order to exist. Tobacco companies need to maintain political control over governments in developing societies. They work to block tobacco-related public health policies. They keep Malawi and other developing societies dependent on tobacco by stoking fear with threatening claims about job losses, cuts in government revenue and the loss of money available for vital social services. What would happen if they declared bankruptcy and went home? Would Malawian landowners treat their workers any differently if they were selling their tobacco to other buyers?

Fieldwork-based money exchanges and corporate malfeasance, I came to think, fell on the same side – the "suspect" side – of the social-responsibility coin. From Eugene's standpoint, they were the same. And from his standpoint, corporate accountability and labor solidarity were the same, too. Yet I held on to the idea that by addressing global inequities, I would erase the necessity to continue my work. In that sense, anyway, I hoped that what I did could be distinguished from a corporate social-responsibility project. Tobacco companies hoped to use corporate social-responsibility projects to preserve themselves and their trade. I hoped to make my own work obsolete.

Postscript

In Spring 2005, the bottom fell out of Malawi's tobacco market. Tobacco prices, which have dropped 50 percent over the last ten years, fell to US$0.80–0.90 per kilogram of dried leaves. In an article about Malawi tobacco growers in the *Guardian* newspaper, a spokesperson for Philip Morris International said, "We do not deal directly with farmers, nor do we own any farms … we are not aware of any changes [in prices] this year."[7]

Notes

1. All of the names used in the chapter are pseudonyms.
2. My first trip to Malawi, a two-month visit in 1995, was made to complete research on textile workers for a degree in labor studies at the Institute of Social Studies in the Hague, the Netherlands. The trips described in this chapter were made as part of work toward a Ph.D. in cultural anthropology at the University of California, Irvine.
3. After I left Malawi, global leaf merchants started to contract directly with tobacco farmers. Philip Morris is the top purchaser of tobacco from Universal Corporation, the global leaf merchant that buys, through its subsidiary, about

50 percent of Malawi's leaf. It issues monthly reports on tobacco prices in Malawi   (www.universalcorp.com/Reports/SelectReport.asp?Menu=Tob& Archive=&ID=1002). An internal Philip Morris document shows that 20 percent of the company's burley tobacco supply derives from Malawi. (Burley is a lighter, nicotine-rich variety of tobacco used as filler in cigarettes. In Malawi, it is grown mainly on smallholder farms.)

4. Identification cards were, historically, a loaded issue. During the one-party rule of Kamuzu Banda (1964–94), people were forced to purchase party cards. This gave low-ranking members of Banda's regime a means to extort money from the general public. Members of Banda's Young Pioneers and Youth League used violence on those who refused to capitulate. Without a party card, ordinary people were denied entrance to markets or access to key roads. Nonetheless, some tobacco workers preferred Banda's regime to the regime of Bakili Muluzi (1994–2004). Banda's regime had at least made identity cards accessible to the ordinary citizens, and gave them a sense of belonging to the state.

5. Now, in my current position as a postdoctoral researcher, I continue to do work to expose the labor abuses of transnational tobacco companies in Africa, and encourage labor participation in policymaking processes on tobacco control and public health.

6. According to the ECLT 2001–2 report, the project in Nkhotakota that employed Eugene was "exceptionally funded by Scandinavian Tobacco through the ECLT Foundation." The report goes on to say, with some anxiety, "All other and future ECLT Foundation projects are to be funded by the Foundation Board members collectively." (www.eclt.org/filestore/ECLTAnnualReport.pdf)

7. John Vidal, "How Malawi's Livelihood Went Up in Smoke," *Guardian*, June 8, 2005.

CHAPTER 6

What Do You Want Me to Do, Bang My Head Against the Wall?

Reflections on Having and Not Having in the Field

Stefan Senders

In 1986 I traveled to Ghana, West Africa, to learn Ewé and Dagbamba drumming. I had studied and played the music in the Boston area for some years, and I had put in my hours transcribing tapes, working with dancers and performing in an excellent Drum and Dance Ensemble. Traveling to Ghana seemed like a logical step. I made arrangements to study with two great players – Godwin Agbeli in Accra, and Fuseni Allhasan in Tamalé – and by performing music, banging nails, borrowing and begging, I gradually accumulated enough money to make the trip last for a few months. I was no trained ethnographer, but I had some experience with fieldwork; I had spent many years playing and studying Appalachian music, and some of that had been under the aegis of a National Endowment for the Arts Apprenticeship Grant. I had done a fair bit of reading, and I had hopes of pursuing a graduate degree in ethnomusicology; I felt like a novice, but not a rank beginner.

Before I left I had been warned not to drink the water, to avoid fresh vegetables, and to carry my money hidden in a money belt. I was to carry a relatively large quantity of small bills – to *dash* (bribe) the officials – and never to carry all my money in one place. I was warned about the taxi drivers, who would overcharge me; the street children, who would pester me with their begging; and the officials, who would try to wring out of me whatever they could. I was told never to change my money in a bank, because I'd get a better rate on the street, and that if I wanted a visa (to travel in Burkina Faso, for example) I'd do better by giving a little money to a friend's girlfriend than to try to work by the rules.

People told me over and over, and with what seemed like great pleasure, about the corruption I would find. I suspect that the corruption was particularly important because it signaled a real difference between "our" society and "theirs." Sure, we have corruption, but it runs underground and is considered an aberration, not the norm.

I didn't have much money but on the day I left for the airport I dutifully tucked what I had into my new money belt, put some small bills in my wallet and, without thinking, put two fifties in my passport. I remembered them only when I got to the airport and the clerk at the airline desk checked my papers: "You'd better not leave these in there!" she said, "They'll think it's for them!" I packed the bills away.

Many hours and changes later, the plane landed in Accra, and along with the other passengers I walked across the hot field and filed into the small concrete terminal. There we were met by two immigration officials who cursorily checked each of our visas and stamped us through. I don't know what they told the other passengers, but when I got to the desk one said, "You know, it's the official's birthday today. I think you should give him a present. Fifty is good." I refused, quietly. They stared, repeated the line, and when I shook my head they let me through. I was really there.

Refusing requests, pleas and demands became a regular and defining feature of my experience in Ghana. I refused to give people my clothes, I refused to marry them, I refused to open import–export businesses with them, I refused to buy them outboard motors. There appeared to be a shared sense that I was an almost limitless source of wealth and goods, and my perceptions of Ghana were powerfully shaped by my new identity – whether through my refusals or my generosity.

I took a cab to the hotel, and I'm sure I overpaid. I took my room – I remember the smells of the charcoal fires behind the building, and the sounds of cars, music and talk in the air. My experience of those moments was heightened, sharp and strange. I had been warned of unsafe hotel rooms and light-fingered maids, so it seemed only natural to bar the door with a chair before I went to sleep. I awoke to two men banging on the door – it was late in the morning and they were worried. I was to meet Godwin, my teacher, that morning at the Arts Council building, which stood about a quarter of a mile away, so I took my bag and set off through the field of bush that lay between the hotel and the Arts Council.

When I found Godwin, he was shocked that I had walked by way of the bush; it was lucky, he said, that I hadn't been robbed or killed. Was it true that this place was so risky? Was I, as a white man, so obviously a target for thieves? I guess they would assume I had money.

It was clear that there was no way to distinguish precisely between my color and my wealth. The two were associated in an inevitable way; the probability that I, a notably white man, was in Ghana with less money than the Ghanaians was extremely low. My relative wealth was obvious.

We ate. We talked. We drank. We drank more. Godwin took me to see the rest of the buildings, and then we set out to his small rooms outside the center of town. He left me with his two children while he took some of my money and went out to find a money-changer. When he returned we arranged that I would give him a relatively large sum of money – a few hundred dollars – which he was to use to pay bribes and other unnamed expenses. He would be my guide. I remember feeling a kind of pleasure – relief really – in relinquishing the responsibility of paying and bribing. It was, I suppose, an attempt to recapture a kind of child-like state in which I would be "taken care of." The metaphor, however, was not entirely mine; Godwin saw himself as my teacher and my caretaker; his role was not far from "father." Moreover, it seemed honest to admit that I was effectively helpless; I could not speak any Ghanaian language, and even though many Accra residents could speak English, I would not, particularly during those first days, have been much good on my own.

A few days later we headed to Godwin's family village. There his family would be able to help me find the *Agbadja* and *Yewe* music I had hoped to hear. Once there, we ate, drank, talked and drank. Godwin again left me in the care of his family while he headed out to "do some business." In the middle of that first night one of Godwin's brothers came to me urgently: "Come! Bring your bag. We have to go. Godwin has said that you must hear what is happening!" Where Godwin was I don't know. And we went running through the moonlit cassava fields. My camera, tape recorder and microphones banged against my hip as we ran. After what seemed a long while we stood outside an enclosed compound; inside I could hear singing and drumming. Godwin's brother asked me to wait while he went inside. He soon returned and said that I would not be allowed in, but that I could record the music from outside the walls. At that point the drumming had picked up considerably – it was cult music. Naively I agreed, and I began to set up the tape recorder.

A few moments later I was jarred from my headphones by two men with machetes. They obviously did not want me there. They wanted, it seemed, to kill me. Godwin's brother frantically explained and cajoled, and finally they agreed – if I would get them a few bottles of gin, then I could come inside and record all the music I wanted. I would even be allowed to see the cult fetish. We set out to find some gin. It wasn't hard. At a nearby hut we were able to purchase a few bottles (I paid). Fifteen minutes later we were back at the compound, and this time I was allowed inside.

It is hard for me to tell, particularly from this vantage, whether I was really in danger. I think I was. At the time it was like a dream: the knives, the threats, all bathed in music and moonlight. To have it so easily recast as a simple act of exchange – gin for life – confirmed the strangeness, both by the very transformation of my life into a commodity, and by the low price bid for it.

For the rest of my time in southern Ghana, in Accra and in the village, I made my introductions and payments – to men – with "gin" or *Akpeteshé*. Before every session we bought gin – we poured libations to call the ancestors, and we drank it "to make us boozed." We arranged gin for the ensemble, and we drank together from the little gin carts that passed by the Center. Alcohol cemented obligations that money could not. Even the owner of the beer stall down the lane insisted on giving me beer, which I'm sure he could hardly afford, but it turned out he expected me to "arrange" a new outboard motor for his fishing boat. The women were not part of the alcohol economy, and for them we (it was I who was paying) bought meat, vegetables or cloth. Many of the women were extremely friendly, and they would tell me in all manner of ways that what they really wanted was for me to marry them and take them for a long plane ride. They liked me, Godwin told me, "because I had a good frame." And besides, "It is good to have another wife."

Twice-marked, I felt profoundly *white*. Outside of a few German tourists, who turned up rarely, I was one of the few non-Africans I saw. And I felt profoundly *rich*. Beggar children occasionally swarmed me on the street, and new acquaintances would make sure I knew of their need for stretch jeans, "converseshoes" and cash. Almost everyone was suffering at the time. Ghana had weathered massive economic decline since the collapse of cocoa prices in the mid-1960s. Unemployment was high and had been exacerbated by the return migration of Ghanaians who had been expelled from Nigeria in 1983. Food had been short in the years prior as a result of drought and fire, and austerity measures adopted as conditions of World Bank loans taken in 1983 only made things worse. It was hard times, and people in Accra were unsure of their future; as one woman admonished me when she heard that I had not been listening to the radio, "But you might come to town and it would be a coup! And the bullets would be flying!"

One day Godwin and I returned to his rooms, and I found that a quantity of bills had been stolen from my bag where I had foolishly left them. Godwin was sure that his children had taken the money. The next night he woke them from sleep and pulled them both into his bedroom. I heard yelling. Crying. Yelling. More crying. The next morning he told me that they had confessed, and that they would return the money. He was ashamed, and he asked my forgiveness. Of course, I responded, but what I really wanted to know was, what had happened in the bedroom? "I beat them," he said in his lovely and endearing falsetto. "I beat them, and then I made them drink something. I told them that if they told a lie they would suffer. They would shit and shit until they died! They told me the truth." It was Juju. Magic of shit and death. Protecting my money.

Money not only allowed me access to events and experiences I might otherwise never have seen, it also precipitated events that would otherwise not have occurred. In a sense, then, money, and my money in particular, was a truly creative force in the creation of the culture I was trying to understand. Juju. Marriage. Shit. Booze. Death.

After a couple of months in Accra, I headed north to Tamalé, where I met Abu Bakkari Lunna, who had agreed to help me. He introduced me to Fuseni Alhassan, a virtuoso player of the GunGon, the Dagbamba bass drum. One morning Abu sent "a small boy" to get Fuseni and his son, and the four of us met in one of Abu's small rooms (Abu was a successful musician, had three wives and was by local standards well-off). Abu explained that I had come to study. Fuseni nodded.

I asked Abu to explain that I had money to offer, that it wasn't much – around US$75 – and that I hoped that would be of some use to him. I remember feeling ashamed to offer so little, but I was quickly running out of cash. My innocence had made my stay in the more expensive south longer than I had anticipated, and the money that I had hoped would arrive by mail had failed to materialize – it had been stolen from the mail and "chopped." I handed Fuseni the money; he accepted it, leaned back, and asked me: "Do you want me to kill myself? What do you want me to do, bang my head against the wall?"

I remember being stunned by such a graphic idiom: was that what I was really buying, a life?

As I got to know more about the life of musicians in Tamale, I came to better understand Fuseni's remark. As musicians, said Abu, we were "like women." We had to come when called and play when asked. But those obligations were implicit, and they were more firmly rooted in "traditional" relations of reciprocity; the money, which I had naively seen as *something apart*, an expression of less intimate relations, showed itself anew and suddenly stripped of its aura.

When I was finally ready to leave Ghana, I spent my last night in Godwin's rooms. Members of his family were visiting, and we were packed four to a room for the night. It was hot, but we kept all the doors and windows boarded – "because of thieves." We slept bathed in sweat. In the morning, both Abu and Godwin saw me to the cab. Abu had traveled all the way from Tamale, a distance of many miles and a grueling bus trip, in hopes of securing some cash he was sure I'd be getting in the mail. It had never arrived – surely stolen and chopped – and he left, frustrated, with a gym bag, towels and a tape recorder. Godwin, I know, had set aside some of the original capital. I wasn't worried about him.

I overpaid the cab driver and took my bags upstairs, where I met the desk official. "Five," he said. "Five anything. Francs, Marks, Dollars. Five." The smallest bill I had was a twenty. I asked him if he had change, but apparently he didn't. On the plane I sat with a young blonde teenager, the daughter of an oil company executive and she complained to me that her time in Ghana had been boring. "There's nothing to do here," she said. "You just can't get *anything.*"

So How Big is Your House? Do You Have *Everything*?

Many years later, at the time I was preparing for my doctoral fieldwork, I was living with my wife, Elizabeth, and our son, Owen, who was about two, in a tiny and rundown farmhouse some miles outside of Ithaca, New York. We had a little garden, a woodstove and lots of squirrels living in the walls. We loved it, but if it sounds too good, let me put it in perspective this way: we were easily approved for the mortgage on nothing but a graduate stipend. Those years were stressful. We were often in debt, and before we could make things change, I had to finish my research. Actually, I needed to begin my research, and that required that I secure funding for the project. I wrote proposals, honed and spun my arguments, and spent a lot of time wondering if the mail had arrived.

As graduate students we rarely, if ever, discussed the ways our finances and funding might shape our research. It was clear enough that without funding the research wouldn't happen, but we maintained what I can only regard as a fictional isolation from the power of money to influence our research questions and practices. There were some exceptions, of course, but they were mostly framed in the negative: "Would you accept money from the Defense Department?"

I did get funding from a variety of sources, but it wasn't much, considering that we were heading for Berlin, Germany, not Indonesia or Thailand. I knew a few graduate students who had set out for research in Southeast Asia; they had nice apartments, had their laundry done for them, and lived in relative luxury. Germany was another story; in 1994 the dollar was close to a postwar low against the deutschmark (DM) and the housing shortage in Berlin, the new *Wohnungsnot* or "housing crisis" had almost reached its apogee. At that time, Berlin was counted "the most expensive city in Europe."

I assume that every field site comes with an associated body of fantasy and advice. Here the main issues were expense and bureaucracy: I was told to expect lots of both.

We were worried, but at least we had already found a place to live. We had heard, through a friend of a friend, of an apartment in Berlin – it would come open just at the time we would arrive; it was in an interesting neighborhood in the West; more important, it was small and cheap. By mail and fax we sublet it, furnished, sight unseen, and we felt relieved. Maybe this was going to work.

The apartment was on the third floor of a *Hinterhaus*, in the back section of an old apartment complex in what residents later told us was the "slum of Charlottenburg." The windows in the stair shaft had all been broken out, and pigeons had taken over; the walk up was to thread through the guano, and to shoo the more belligerent of the birds out of the way.

We had heard that the apartment was small, and that it wasn't particularly pleasant, but we were not quite prepared for what we found. It was one room about twelve feet square. Off one corner of the room was a minute kitchenette, and in what must have been a former closet was the bath. The bed was an old folding leatherette couch, and the only other furniture in the room was a decrepit "armoire," a small desk, and a huge TV that dominated the room.

Two big windows opened onto the inner courtyard, where on some days we could see the refugee children from the asylum dormitory in the back beating the rats, which staggered, riddled with poison, out into gutters to die. From the cheap bakery on the ground floor, the place smelled alternately of pastry crème and rotting garbage. I know this must sound like a parody, sort of a "down and out in Berlin," but if anything, I underplay the scene.

I compare my situations in Berlin and Ithaca. Why, it is worth asking, was one more bearable than the other? In Ithaca we lived in the country and we had plenty of outside space, a garden, and a kind of solace in the pastoral beauty that surrounded us. In Berlin, by contrast, we were relatively isolated in a back alley, and there was no relief either within the apartment or outside its windows. We always tried to get away from the place, not back to it.

The apartment was awful, but it still ate up much of our available money. We were stretched thin in any case – our visas prevented us from working, and that left us to support two adults, one child and a dog (I had not mentioned Emily's food in our budget request) on a single graduate research budget. We began searching for a new place immediately, but the market was exceedingly tight. We began to get depressed.

Because we were strapped, it was difficult for me to get out to meet the people I needed to meet. I felt constrained; the cost of transportation, food, gifts – each research step was a matter of calculation. When I was out, moreover, I was always concerned about my family's increasing malaise. I did not have the aura of power that is so helpful to the anthropologist, and I know I seemed unlikely and out of place. Some of my initial contacts were sure I was either working some kind of insurance scam – they were the marks, presumably – or that I was a government spy interested in the legitimacy of their immigration claims.

We did find another apartment, and even though it meant going deeply into debt, we took it. Eventually I was able to make a good many contacts and to get my research going. Ultimately, I found that money, and specifically my lack of it, proved central, not ancillary, to my work. I had come to Berlin to work with *Aussiedler*, repatriating "ethnic Germans" from Central Asia and Siberia. Like many immigrants, they had left behind much of what wealth they had, and they were trying to make their way, economically as well as culturally, in their new *"alte Heimat."* They were, to put it plainly, almost as broke as I was.

It is arguable that the comparison is illegitimate, that while I didn't have much money, I did have access to the American economy, to graduate education, to English – all assets usually seen as valuable. But my position as "anthropologist," while it had a ring of professionalism about it, was consistently undermined by my day-to-day finances; the issue, in other words, had less to do with wealth than it did with money.

In some respects, in fact, they were even better off than I was. They were allowed to work, they received special state benefits, and they had a large community of churches, charities and community groups who worked to help them. I had none of those things going for me.

I sat, ate, walked and drank with Aussiedler; we painted walls, waited in offices and we talked. Talked about money, about work and about the future. We planned and strategized – how to find a cheaper apartment, how to manage the bureaucracy. Some assumed that because I was an American, I was rich, and that I could navigate the bureaucracy with ease, backed by the power of my passport. As a representative of the United States, I played an important role in their fantasies of the future; for them, the USA signified the redemptive power of capitalism; it was truly a land of *Dallas* and dollars, a fantasy landscape, a future dream.

One afternoon I sat with Alex, Irma and Liza, three Aussiedler from Siberia and Kazakhstan, and we were passing around photos of the houses they had left behind. Then they asked about me. How big is your house? I showed them pictures – of snow, the old metal roof and leaky windows. But what about the kitchen, they wondered. Is it big? With lots of modern appliances? *Do you have everything?*

CHAPTER 7

Circuits of Conversion

From 14,000 to 1

Naeem Inayatullah

Money, like economics, produces considerable anxiety for many of us. To address it I need to speak about *price* and *value* – two concepts I have been struggling to understand most of my life. Further, I cannot seem to speak about any of these terms without working my way through another notoriously difficult concept, namely gravity. Allow me to start with gravity.

Mersing, as I remember it from my visit in late 1979, was a small and picturesque fishing village northeast of Singapore and Johor Baharu, Malaysia. Nan Bonfils and I were there at the invitation of Jim Baker, son to generations of missionaries working in Malaysia and Indonesia. Jim thrived on all things Malay and lived so that each of his actions would respect and cultivate aspects of local culture. He was a kind of an anti-missionary trying to undo the damage done by his relatives. Nan and Jim were teachers at the International School of Kuala Lumpur. I fell in with them as a regular substitute teacher while searching for employment after having earned a Master's in economics. Our destination was a forty-five-minute boat ride east of Mersing toward one of the smaller islands, where Jim's family owned a house.

When our chartered fishing boat arrived on Babi Hijong we could still not see the four houses on the island. But as the sand absorbed our feet and as we unloaded food supplies, Nan and I beamed mirrored grins. We had somehow dropped into a dream – a tropical island in the South China Sea, complete with swaying trees, a lush green interior, a double coral reef – all provided by a gracious and trustworthy guide. We three were the only inhabitants on the island – left there without the distractions of electricity, plumbing, radios or phones.

In the morning, I thought I heard the echoes of a megaphone. Could I hear noise from the mainland so many miles out, I asked. Jim pointed to the next island. It was within swimming distance. He explained that his family house had originally been located on the bigger island but they had been forced to relocate after the arrival of more than nine thousand "Vietnamese boat people" – ethnic Chinese fleeing Vietnam who the Malaysian government refused to allow on the mainland. The government feared that these additional Chinese might trigger violence within the already volatile cultural political economy of the peninsula. The megaphone I heard was part of a UN relief effort.

As I listened I pondered the juxtaposition: they, 9,000 boat people on that island quarantined, waiting urgently and anxiously to hear of their relocation to somewhere on the planet; we three on this island, lying on the beach, cleansing ourselves of everyday toxins. Heaven and hell always appear together.

Gravity. I am still coming to that. Ideas, like the wind in my hair, flowed through my mind as I sat on the beach each day. I felt grounded as I observed each sunrise and sunset, witnessed the moon rise and set. Surrounded by the sea and its tides, I effortlessly ignored our neighboring island. As the sun set to the west over Mersing, I saw the moon's light change from the distant flatness it offers during the day to that golden three dimensionality it reflects at twilight. Then it occurred to me: the moon is, in fact, reflecting the light of the sun. I could trace the vectors of light with my fingers: the sun sending light in all directions, that light bouncing off the surface of the moon, and coming down to my eyes on the beach. For the first time I saw the moon as a three-dimensional object, as something floating in space. There was more. An object that large – just hanging there – had to affect the tides as it moved in its orbit. I saw that; felt and sensed it. I was euphoric because I had intuited the effects of gravity.

Recently, twenty-six years later, I resumed that reflection on the big island of Hawaii. I had seen the oozing lava, the newly created black sand beaches where two-foot waves battered me. And there again were the sun, the moon, the tides and gravity. I still don't know the exact details of this system of interrelations, but I think I know something more than I did a quarter century ago. That more is this: concrete expressions vivify abstractions; the seemingly random material of actual experience emerges as already moving within a systematic dynamic whole. Transcendence and imminence work through each other – they differ in name and function, but both work seamlessly as one.

Meaning what exactly? And why mention it? Because, if the concepts that we use to explain the world are productive of understanding, then those concepts cannot be altogether separate from the existent processes they help to elucidate. The concepts and the processes are two aspects of one reality.

I don't know how to express the significance of this claim. I wish I could say it simply and forcefully. Maybe I can give you a better sense of it if I shift from tides, waves and gravity to money, value and price.

My recent trip to Pakistan was not without some small element of success – with a book coming out, tenure around the bend at a liberal arts college, and some long-term financial hope of supporting my immediate family of four. This trip differed from my home visits as a child, teenager and young adult. Then it was my parents' money that paid for everything – the trips themselves, my clothes and the large number of gifts I always purchased. One thing that had not changed was the need to translate dollars into rupees. This always requires a similar set of operations, namely, conversions and calculations. Conversion from dollars to rupees, from the 1:5 in the 1960s to the current 1:60; and calculations that translate dollars into gifts for my friends – kurtas, brass lamps, pillow cases, artisanal ware – things I hoped would allow my friends to believe that elsewhere, further than the dark side of the moon, life was also being lived. My college roommate Ted once teased, "How do we know you have a family in Pakistan? Or, that you have ever been there? For all we know you could be a CIA plant!" Pakistanis, on the other hand, had few doubts about America's existence. Just questions about how much of it I had brought back to them: "Can you do the twist? What kinds of cars have you ridden? Did you bring the latest Beatles album?"

Returning to Pakistan with a U.S. job triggers two questions – inescapable and mandatory: "What work do you do?" and "How much money do you make?" Except some family and a masseur from China, no one seems impressed that I am a paid "scholar." In any case, the query about occupation is merely the opening to the real line of inquiry. My first decision – I have not yet settled on a formula – is whether or not I will offer some vague and diffuse answer about my salary. Declining this question provides insult and merely delays the matter. Giving offense is no small consideration since the primary mode of social relation is familial – acquaintanceship assumes friendship, friendship implies family; family is embedded in obligation, responsibility and (seeming) open access. Hence, shortly after names have been exchanged, one can expect questions about land, size of home, salary and connections to the wealthy and powerful. Vagueness in response is permissible; annoyance is not.

Feeling that I can no longer participate in the veiling of material life, I sometimes give a number – especially when I am deep in the heart of the Punjab's agrarian terrain where my romantic link with the land has me at ease and unguarded. Except for one instance that I will relate shortly, the conversations have a set pattern. I give the number, say $30,000 (back in the days when Assistant Professors in the social sciences started at less than thirty thousand). Converted by a factor of thirty, fifty or sixty, depending on the year, the sum in rupees is a fortune. At that moment many things happen simultaneously. First, my co-conversationalist begins to imagine what he (always a he – I have never had this conversation with a woman) could do with such a sum and what I must be doing with it. I have learned to wait as this fantasy takes flight. My silence and stoic posture brings him back to the moment. I wait for the next two comments: "*Mahshalla* [thanks be to God] you are a wealthy man." I suspect that it is important to share in this vicarious pride – I want him to feel this success because it is also his; he and I look the same, have emerged from the same land. And then it comes.

Whether this is a moment of illusion or transparency, I leave to you: "How fortunate you are to live in America." This conversion of value I cannot accept without generating a counter circulation.

I begin my response with the hidden balance of the other side of the ledger: translated into rupees the dollar cost of living – rent and food – is equally unfathomable. In my accounting I make it nearly impossible to make ends meet on $30,000. I start to lay down the trump cards – how most everyone in the U.S. lives on credit. And then, finally, quality of life: food tastes better here, I say; there is more vibrancy, more life here, I say; there is more vitality here, I say. The loneliness of an atomized and alienated life is as pervasive there, I try to explain, as color, smell, texture and family are overpowering here.

Quiet for a moment, I know I have not prevailed. The rebuttal: he cites cases of people gone abroad who bring back savings and live in luxury. My turn: but these are the rare cases that have saved money day to day by living as paupers abroad. By sheer luck and determination these few have overcome what most of the others have not, namely loneliness and its symptoms – gambling, booze, drugs, prostitution, television, religion, consumerism and cultural paralysis. What they earn by alienating their labor only feeds that alienation. But he also has a trump card. He surveys my face and declares, "but *you* seem just fine." He does not say this with words but with his bodily dismissal of my failed attempt to puncture his hopes.

Perhaps the most interesting part of this frequent exchange is that it takes place, as economists say, behind both our backs. I do not know why I am trying to deflate his hopes and I suspect that he does not know why he looks toward gold mountains to realize his. There is something of waves, tides and the moon in all this that I am trying to grasp.

I remember the day when I became aware of my role in this subconscious pantomime. It was after a half-day drive from megalopolis of Lahore, beyond my mother's bustling village, in the flat green plains of Punjab. I arrived in a village of no more than ten to twelve homes. In the ensuing clear winter morning I had the usual conversation with one of the villagers about salary – but there was a twist. My trump card was followed by a detailed logistical and monetary explanation of how to enter the USA "illegally," how many years it would take to save money by driving a taxi, and where he was going to buy his house when he returned. He was modeling his plan after someone who had accomplished just this; someone who now lived in a fine brick house in a nearby town. This was a strategy, not a daydream. He wasn't engaged in banter; he was looking to me as a potential contact on the inside.

In my wavering about whether to offer him my address and phone number, it occurred to me that I was playing the role I detest the most, that of the immigrant who, as last one in, is the first to shut the door. I knew that in the actual world, capital circulates *with* the currents while labor swims *against* them. Why, I asked myself, had I been working against his labor, his motion? In the future, I imagine being more supportive. Still I suspect I will hesitate to become an inside contact furthering his mobility since my fear of the Immigration and Naturalization Service (INS) is something my body cannot shake

As a nine-year-old in 1965 Bloomington, Indiana, I delivered papers for a newly started daily. Sundays I made my rounds twice, first early in the morning for the fat weekly edition, and then later on for collection. Collection required a six-by-four-inch book with two rings containing pages of perforated tabs. On top of each page was the name and address of each customer and on the bottom were the tabs marked with weekly dates. I knocked on doors, and waited for the Indiana University graduate students to come to the door. Then I announced "collect," and waited for the money. I carefully tore out the tabs giving one for each week paid. All the money went to the man who hired me. He would pay me the fifteen or so dollars we – he, my parents and I – had agreed. The problem was that in the first three weeks I received no wages. Not that I minded the absence since my direct relationship to money revolved around finding empty soda bottles to return to the IGA grocer on 10th street where I converted them to Tootsie-Rolls, Clark candy bars and the occasional bottle of grape Fanta. When eventually I was paid, I routinely gave it all to my mother. Fifteen dollars a week was a significant sum, given that our whole family lived on my father's graduate student stipend. My paper route probably supplied most of my mother's discretionary income.

I had the sense, though, that the man from the *Tribune* was exploiting me. Perhaps my collection money was all the discretionary income *he* had, I don't know. I said nothing to my parents accepting that his betrayal somehow seeped into me as my shame. In the fourth week my silent endurance was rewarded with pay and then by my mother's grateful smiles. In addition, I started to win prizes – or at least this is what the man from the *Tribune* said. He brought me a baseball glove, a rain jacket and even a twenty-pound turkey. I am convinced that I didn't win the competitions as the *Tribune* man claimed; he was paying interest on my inability to sound off on his original cheating. What saved the day was that I enjoyed the work and had no conception of the meaning of US$15 a week. I was still looking for empty bottles near the railroad tracks.

My friend Paul, another college roommate, told me about his paper delivery business as an adolescent. In the suburbs of Detroit, he sublet two routes to kids in his neighborhood. He collected not by knocking on doors but by mailing bills with stamped return envelopes. In fact, he never left his house. He claimed to be saving for hiking and scuba equipment, but I think his deeper motivation was the magic of making money appear. Appear and multiply.

The most sophisticated beggars in Pakistan are those who come to your house. If the gate is open, they will sit down so that driving a car out of the driveway is possible only with attentive navigation. After the obligatory opening round – the asking and receiving of water, and perhaps some food – the burka-clad woman will announce that she is not leaving until someone in the house gives her enough money to feed her three little children. One of them might be in her lap. The pressure falls on my mother who as the everyday accountant for the household has to make the decision. Her empathy for the poor has not diminished with age or with the rise in our family status. I recall the day she, our cook and the woman who cleaned our toilets all sat and wept when the latter finally confronted my mother with the reality that our practice of throwing out three-day-old rice was a crime against her needs.

But with a professional beggar the context is more strategic. This beggar knows that playing to heartstrings, while an absolutely necessary part of the drama, is insufficient. Hence the strategic deployment of her body in the driveway. The test of nerve and patience will last hours because no one in the house will dare to physically remove her – not even the police. From my mother's point of view, the monetary sum necessary to get rid of the beggar, a negotiation that will take at least a half hour, amounts to little. The real cost is information – paying her will mark our house as vulnerable and place it on the itinerary of the high-end high-risk beggars. If by chance guests are due to arrive, she will risk future annoyance for immediate results. Otherwise, this battle can take the better part of a day. At best the beggar will leave after three or four hours but not without forcing hearts to weaken and harden against the structural and strategic imperatives of sustaining a life of differential wealth. I have watched such battles, unable to imagine a way through this impasse.

I am waiting in the transit lounge for a midnight flight from Islamabad to JFK. Having run the gauntlet of forms, passports, luggage, droves of people and my peaking anxiety that all this should go smoothly, I finally sit and exhale. With the flight still more than an hour away, I think about what I should do with the last 2,000 rupees left in my wallet. The currency exchanger will not convert them to dollars in New York – this I know. Either I spend it in this lounge or they will become tokens along with all the other bills in the top drawer of my desk. To my excitement I discover that there is a small shop that sells CDs and DVDs. I wake up the young attendant, who is bemused that I am a collector of classical Pakistani music. I ask his advice about every recording in the shop. Forty-five minutes latter, with help from his tastes and knowledge, I select some CDs and pay him. He has been waiting for this moment. Handing back my change, he asks me what I will do with the remaining 400 rupees.

He has guessed that they will end up out of circulation. I have no idea of his income, or how much of his wages are made up by offering to relieve travelers of their petty cash. I should just give him the bills, I think. Another part of me hesitates. Am I damaging the local economy by treating what is a significant amount here as if it were spare change? On the other hand, perhaps I am using this ethno-economistic rationale about the disruption of local economies in order to justify my deeper commitments to an economy of just deserts. Beyond asking me for money, did he do anything to deserve the rupees? How did he get a job in a transit lounge anyway? Whom did he have to bribe? Was the expectation of petty cash calculated as a part of his salary? Then, in the see-sawing, I think: Oh come on, you spent your whole career fighting this attitude theoretically and practically – just let go of the bills and don't worry about desert since you have no real idea of how this money came to be in your hands in the first place.

All this transpires in my moment of indecision as he and I sustain eye contact – the only real moment of our encounter. I walk away without a word. On the plane, looking down at the Hindu Kush mountains below, I conclude that I am a fraud.

Money measures value and price like an enormous vertical ruler on a dock measures gravity and the motion of water.

Price and value engage in a necessary tension. Price concretely expresses and actualizes the abstraction value. Properly deciphered, price indicates a particular commodity's role and place in the dynamic flux of a system of commodities – a system whose drive and teleological mission is to generate profit. It is not as simple as a high price generating more profit and a low price generating little, since we know that an airplane carrying 800 passengers might be a future bust and that cotton socks sold in great volume by K-Mart may generate adequate revenue. The complexity of value cannot be grasped from a cursory reading of price. Rather, value is the abstraction that points toward the fuller articulation of the laws and processes of global capitalism. Value is the anticipation of a commodity's relation to all other commodities, to the structured and changing needs of global beings, to the commodity's eventual ability to serve the purpose for which it was made – profit-creation. Value is that anticipation, that process and its realization.

Value is to price as gravity is to the movement of natural objects. To measure the movement of objects we use various types of rulers. Tidal movement is measured in inches and feet, centimeters and meters of displaced ocean water. Displaced water indicates, expresses, actualizes, concretizes and operationalizes the abstraction – gravity. We have three separable elements: the abstraction, gravity; its expression, motion; and that which measure them both, rulers. Likewise with capitalism: we have the abstraction, value; its expression, price; and their measure, money.

Money measures price and value.

If we humans use our self-consciousness and creative energy in order to learn nature's laws and then manipulate them for our own needs, it may also be the case that, from another angle, nature develops the human species so that nature can actualize itself as a self-conscious entity. As for nature so for capitalism: if from one angle we humans generate a social system propelled by profit for the purposes of creating wealth, from another angle, wealth, for the purposes of expanding its self-generation, uses, perhaps even consumes, humans. From this admittedly objectified angle, wealth's productive consumption of humans – which does not necessarily mean their death but merely their post-consumption recycling for the next round of consumption and profit (think of the recycling of soda bottles) – suggests that, as productive inputs in a system of wealth generation, different humans have different values and prices.

To venture into the realm of the value and price of human beings is to enter a foundational debate in political economy. Are humans only slightly different from anything else made for use and therefore commodifiable? Or, is it a category mistake to think of humans as quasi-commodities – a mistake made and hidden in order to thrust humans into a commodity system and make them into a kind of object-being? Or can we temporarily tolerate this human-object tension in the ontologizing of our species for the promise of greater future good, namely wealth? Today, such questions – part of the core of what political economy once was – are largely suppressed. I mention this suppression here not as a critique but as an unadorned claim about the difficulty/impossibility of facing the real.

And yet, we may argue that the need to avoid the real depends on its pervasive mundane presence. Consider the following bits reported in various newspapers.

Janelle Brown reporting for Salon.com in a January 2, 2002 article titled, "The Impossible Calculus of Loss" asks:

> Is the life of an investment banker who died in the World Trade Center worth US$1.65 million in taxpayer money? What about US$3 million? Is the life of a firefighter worth more than that of a janitor he tried to save? How about the life of a woman who died in the Oklahoma City bombing?

Ascertaining the relative worth of these roles, instead of being a hypothetical exercise in a typical philosophy course, is saturated with immediacy because someone will have to make a decision about how to distribute the windfall designated for the victims of 9/11. What Janelle Brown does not notice is that against her will and against the current of dominant ideology, this news is forcing her to assess the price and value of types of human lives. Here are the numbers as she reports them: the

federal payout alone – that is, not including the sums accumulated by
charities and private donations which would double the federal payout –
amounts to an average of US$1.65 million for "each injured or dead
victim." The exact formula for determining how much each victim is
worth is particularized, therefore complex. The determining formula
creates what David Barstow and Diana B. Henriques, in their December
2, 2001 *New York Times* article titled "Gifts for Rescuers Divide Terror
Victims' Families," call "an aristocracy of grief." Whether this "aristocracy
of grief" is better articulated as a "hierarchy of value" is to quibble somewhat. It is also to miss the larger point, namely, that their article expresses
precise assessments of value, price and money. It reports, that is, on the
calculation of the relative worth of lives ended or damaged on 9/11/2001
in New York City.

The average value of firefighters, policemen, janitors, stockbrokers, CIA
agents and CEOs lead to their average price – somewhere upwards of
US$1.65 million. A part of us objects to this number, feeling that humans
cannot be commodified. We want to declare that not that sum, not a thousand times that sum, can state the value of those we love. And yet despite
such remonstration, the number 1.65 million does tell us something,
doesn't it?

At the end of her article Janelle Brown quotes the philosopher Peter
Singer,

> What concerns me the most is the discrepancy in the way people respond to
> appeals to give to Americans [versus] the way they respond to give to people in
> need elsewhere in the world ... [t]his is a particularly glaring case of it, because
> of all the publicity. It may seem hard to say this, but the number of people
> worldwide who died from avoidable causes on Sept. 11 were vastly greater than
> the number of people who died from the attacks ... Americans can be generous,
> but their response is narrow.

Brown's use of Singer's claim, while seemingly plain as daylight, hides a
bit of significant reality behind its Kantian moralism. This bit of reality, for
those of us who have sensed it but never quite believed in our ability to
locate it, provides a peculiar but real satisfaction. Consider, please, the following story from the online edition of a Pakistani paper, *The News*, issued
on July 8, 2002:

> Dehrawad, Afghanistan: The victims of a U.S. air-raid that killed 48 guests and
> wounded 118 at a wedding party in Afghanistan were paid a total of US$18,500
> in compensation [by the U.S.], an official here said ... District commissioner

Abdur Rahim said he paid out to relatives eight million afghanis (US$200) on behalf of each individual killed and three million (US$75) for each wounded person.

At 40,000 afghanis[2] to a dollar, this amounts to 66 billion afghanis per victim of the WTC attack. Or, if we prefer the conversion into what is known as "hard currency": US$1,650,000 for each victim of WTC versus US$112 for each victim of the wedding bombing.

Perhaps ratios rather than raw numbers are more illuminating: dividing 1.65 million by 112 we arrive at 14,732. The last is the number by which we have to multiply the value/price of an Afghan victim in Afghanistan to arrive at the value/price of a victim of the WTC. Rounding down instead of up – although we should round up since the US$1.65 million is only the federal allotment to the victims of WTC – we can arrive at the following proposition: the worth of a WTC victim is 14,000 times greater than that of an Afghan. Fourteen thousand.

First a few details before we get down to what this means, if it means anything:

1. The ratio of 14,000:1 is more likely to be doubled, given that charitable and private contributions were also in the billions of dollars.
2. Strictly speaking not every victim of the WTC was a U.S. citizen; therefore, we cannot claim that the worth of a U.S. citizen is 14,000 to 28,000 times greater than that of an Afghan, not without more precision and many more calculations.
3. Still, these numbers, if not exact, give us an impressionistic sense of how these monetary calculations indicate relative value and price.

Then again perhaps these numbers and ratios mean nothing. I embrace this conclusion since I am moved by Karl Polanyi's claim that we cannot commodify humans without violating them. Nevertheless, let's play this out on the terms of the dominant political economy and see what happens. First, 14,000 seems arbitrary and nonsensical since the issue seems qualitative, not quantitative. If we listen to our heart of hearts we sense that the exact numbers don't really matter. Indeed, it is precisely the deep qualitative discrepancy in relative human value that allows a cataclysmic uproar for those killed on 9/11. This event, if seen say from the point of view of a typical Guatemalan, a Vietnamese, an Iraqi or the average inhabitant of this planet, remains a relatively minor tragedy.[3] Meanwhile, the same discrepancy in value anesthetizes our outrage and short-circuits our empathy, binding us to the cold mathematics that make the wedding bombings as well as near genocides visited upon others elsewhere a mundane feature of doing "business as usual" in the modern world.

Second, and more important, the displacement of water caused by the tides, caused by the moon, caused by the system of planetary motion, is there for all to observe and measure. So also for the displacement of human value – all of us bear witness to it. Indeed, we can measure it. Measuring this displacement is an act that need not spring from a moral motive; rather, in doing so I am performing the scientific part of my education. It's a training that asks me not to be awed by the sheer power of natural or social systems; at the very least I am hoping to dampen their sensational effects on my focus. The effects of the tides, the effects of the relative social worth of New Yorkers and Afghans are here, there and everywhere – ever present in their monotonous banality. I am just trying to measure them.

Perhaps I am being a poor scientist – please feel free to offer your assessment. Perhaps your critique will point to my errors and sharpen my analysis. Nevertheless, until then, and with your permission, I want to share what I can deduce so far. Here are four abstractions:

1. A global social system based on the growth of wealth through private profit-seeking and based on the division of the world into a set of nations treated as states is likely to evaluate the people of these nations on the basis of their relative usefulness in generating profit.
2. Such evaluations do not remain within their nation-state containers. Instead, they are likely to seep into assessments not only of peoples' profit-generating potential (that is, how they might be deployed or consumed in this or that social regime), but also as an assessment of their very being.
3. Those who want to increase (or in some rare cases, decrease) their self-worth will attempt to move across national boundaries – boundaries that, among other things, indicate and mark relative value.
4. Such assessments of relative worth are expressed in existent reality.

If so, these expressions can be gleaned and measured. They can be observed in the stories I have been telling about money. And perhaps in other stories you might share.

Without knowing it, we monetize ourselves – making ourselves into a measure of value, seeking to circulate ourselves into a different displacement of worth and blocking those who seek to flow upstream (and sometimes downstream). Supporting the status quo in this way seems normal because challenging this normality requires having intuited and opposed the rules and flows of the current social system.

Encounters with money, of the type I have related, appear to be stutters, hesitations, glitches in our ethical self-consciousness when we have not yet worked out whether our particular acts work to valorize or work to counter ratios such as 14,000:1.

My friend Nan left Colorado for Africa one winter. Buried under ten feet of snow in Fairplay's library and powerless against the cold Colorado winds, Nan pushed to the warmth of her deeper desire. She answered an ad for a grade-school teacher. Following a transatlantic agreement over the phone, and having spent her own money for the flight, she arrived in Kinshasa. She had never left the country and knew little more about Zaire other than it would be hot, lush and more attuned to what she hoped to become. Ten years later, in Kuala Lumpur, where we met, she was a veteran of the international school circuit, a circuit through which teachers tour the world by changing schools every two or three years.

After a few notches in her tour, Nan had settled on the International School of Kuala Lumpur where she was a "foreign hire." The designation does not come with merely being a foreigner since there were plenty of those on "local" contracts. It meant that she would be paid in U.S. dollars, would receive a housing allowance, and would be supplied with a roundtrip ticket to the U.S. every two years. Local hires in contrast were paid in Malaysian ringgits with no additional benefits. In 1980, her hard currency pay was US$20,000. She was able to place all of her income in savings because she used her housing allowance to pay rent, food and her other bills. Relative to American/European standards she rented a small track bungalow with two bedrooms, living room, kitchen and a front yard the size of half a badminton court. Middle-class Malaysians who lived four and six in the same sized units surrounded her. She loved her neighborhood and rode her bicycle for transport.

By spending her non-working hours in the local economy while being remunerated at the level of an ex-patriot, Nan was quickly able to build up her savings. Indeed, diversifying her portfolio so that it included, for example, stocks and gems, became one of her minor worries. On the whole, however, the accumulation of wealth was a distant concern; Nan loved teaching, loved Malaysia's flora, fauna, food, and loved most of all being enfolded within its people – Malays, Chinese, Indians. They massaged the stiffness and soothed the aches caused by her slightly aristocratic New England upbringing and by the chill of Rocky Mountain winters.

Of course, Nan's strategy of going native came with a diminution of status – nothing could be done about this displacement. This change failed to curtail Nan since her value polarities were inverted – she needed Malaysia much more than the U.S. In any case, the dollar community did not reject her outright since she had their children for the better part of each week. In addition, Nan's grounded gregariousness, subtle humor and vital and sincere social grace give her equal access to ex-pats and locals. But best of all for Nan was that there was a small group of ISKL teachers who, like her, were converting to locality. Of these, Terry was a Peace Corps volunteer who had become a grade-school teacher.

Terry was harder for me to engage or understand. We shared a quiet understanding that we were moving in opposite directions. For reasons that I did not have the opportunity to explore, he had a need to eradicate all traces of his American past. His going native went as far, perhaps, as one could go: a conversion to Islam, circulating exclusively in his off-hours with Malays, dressing in local fashion at every occasion, a natural change in his accent to the tonalities, rhythms and textures of Malaysian English, and dreaming not in English but in Malay. Indeed, it was my understanding that he had forfeited his U.S. passport in order to become a Malaysian citizen.

While Terry's name did not usually come up in my conversations with Nan, his example often did. My conversations with Nan were far-ranging but always energized by the tensions created by the framework of cultural encounter. Her conversion to Islam played a part in my mother's and our family's open embrace of her. But mostly she was able to relax us with her willingness to enter our house and fully accept the pathologies of our family life as ordinary, without need for comment or adjustment. While sipping lime juice with soda and eating *sate* at some street side stall, our conversations often turned to the theme of conversion. I would ask her what she gained in Islam that she could not find in Catholicism. Having been the target of both Christian and Muslim evangelizing, I could not imagine formally committing to either institution. Her answer stays with me as a puzzle: "It's a straighter shot to God," she said. I am still pondering this linear image. Her question to me has also stayed. It had to do with Terry's wager. She asked, "Do you think I should give up my passport and apply for Malaysian citizenship?"

I never considered becoming Malaysian even though, much like Nan, I am enamored of Malaysia. I will confess, however, that I have harbored a conversionary impulse aimed at bringing out the Afghan in me. I continue to feel a great pull towards Afghanistan. This confession, having come to the surface through this writing, makes me wonder: If some desire circulates in one direction to make up the 14,000: 1 deficit, and other desires circulate in the opposite direction, does this mean that there is also 14,000: 1 ratio that works the other way? What do they have there that is 14,000 times greater than what I can get here? How do I make up that deficit?

Bibliographic Note

The "circuits of conversion" imagery comes directly from Chapter 1, of Marx's *Capital*. My understanding of the relationship between value, price and money is influenced by a reading of Adam Smith's and Karl Marx's analysis of the labor theory of value. That reading has been largely determined by David P. Levine's Hegelian reading of Smith and Marx in the following books: *Economic Studies: Contributions to the Critique of Political Economy* (Routledge Kegan and Paul, 1977) and *Economic Theory: The Elementary Relations of Economic Life, Volume I* (Routledge Kegan and Paul, 1978).

My other main source is what we usually call "auto-biographical." In academic circles autobiography is unfortunately and unselfconsciously thought to be self-indulgent. To counter this bias, I want to move away from this term and toward the idea that we can read lives and consider them as sources. Autobiography can be seen as a "primary self-source" where biographies and interviews would be "secondary self-sources." The retrospective and continuous reading of a person's life – even one's own – while different from reading a text is perhaps neither more nor less reliable a source. Reading a life, like reading a text, can range from being mechanical, simplistic and facile to being theorized, contextualized and insightful.

Notes

1. I am grateful to David Blaney, Nan Bonfils, Beverly DiCocco, Debbie Lisle, Lisa Loomis, Laura McNeal, Stefan Senders and Allison Truitt. Each provided detailed comments and/or pointed to problems that remain difficult for me to solve in this space. The essay is dedicated to the memory of Terry.

2. It is a fortuitous accident for my purposes that Afghans are called Afghanis in the Western press, that is, the national identity is conflated with the national measure of value; like calling citizens of the U.S. "dollars" – something local sources would never confuse.

3. What remains to me a hyperbolic response offered to the 9/11 massacre by most – but certainly not all – citizens of the U.S., can I think be explained by two factors: an immediate, deeply enabling, but mostly novel openness to the possibility that, "there but for the grace of circumstance go I," and the presence of video cameras. Imagine these two elements being equally available for say, the fire-bombing of Dresden, the bombing of Hiroshima, and the napalming of Vietnam. Or with faster camera speeds: the slave ships during the middle voyage, the late-nineteenth-century planned famines of British India, or, to stay within the political landscape of the U.S., General Sherman's march through the South. Deploying our imagination in this way may allow us to grasp the material smallness of the 9/11 massacre and the gargantuan proportions of current U.S. self-aggrandizement. Here, finally, the number 14,000 seems appropriate.

CHAPTER 8

Guide to Further Reading

This Guide to Further Reading is intended to introduce students to anthropological literature on money. It is not an exhaustive survey, but we hope it will offer interested readers a starting point for inquiry. Along the way, it positions the essays of this volume within conversations about what money means and what money does.

We introduced the volume with the disclaimer that our objective was not to produce an "anthropology of money." Our concern has been less about money and more with how "encounters" with money produce anthropological understanding. While people transact with money all the time, not all such transactions generate what we have called "encounter." For ethnographers, money is often a source of both knowledge and trouble; because money tends to be deeply symbolic and subtly coded, it offers ethnographers remarkable insights into local cultures. At the same time, it also offers numerous opportunities for failures – of reading, of acting, of responsibility.

Students who are interested in histories of money can read Jack Weatherford's *The History of Money* (1998), James Buchanan's *Frozen Desire* (1997) or Thomas Crump's *The Phenomenon of Money* (1981). For an astute analysis of how anthropologists are influenced by Western folk theories of money, see Keith Hart's *Money in an Unequal World* (2001). An abbreviated version of his insights can be found in his "Notes Towards an Anthropology of Money" (2005), a refreshing analysis of the widespread idea that money originates in barter, and the popular claim that money undermines traditional cultures. Bill Maurer's (2006) recent review of anthropological research on money and finance examines several distinctive qualities attributed to modern money, including commensuration, abstraction, quantification and reification. As well, in his recent ethnography on Islamic banking and local currencies, Maurer

(2005) demonstrates a novel analytical practice of "lateral reason" for understanding the generation of knowledge.

In addition to these overviews, there are several notable ethnographic collections on money. J. Parry and M. Bloch's *Money and the Morality of Exchange* (1989) offers ethnographic studies that contradict prevailing beliefs of how money gives rise to a particular world view. They argue instead that "an existing world view gives rise to particular ways of representing money" (1989: 19). Furthermore, the moral valuation of money should be understood, not in terms of short-term acquisition, but in terms of "transactional systems," long-term reproduction of social relations (23). Two additional collections are J. Robbins' and D. Akin's *Money and Modernity* (1999) and J. Guyer's *Money Matters: Instability, Values, and Social Payments in the Modern History of West African Communities* (1994a). The essays in the former volume are detailed ethnographic studies of local currencies that have not been wholly subsumed by state-issued currencies. The latter volume examines the ways ordinary people conceptualize money and it illuminates their innovations in its use as a social payment. Both volumes show the complex interaction of local and international monetary systems that animate the valuation and evaluation of currency.

Ethnographic studies of money have, by and large, focused on non-Western societies. This focus has led anthropologists to emphasize the differences among people in their conceptualizations of money, an emphasis that is a hallmark of anthropological thought. As we argued in the introduction, this tendency has led anthropologists to overlook how money shapes their own encounters in the field. Mary Douglas (1958) and E. E. Evans-Pritchard (1940) may not have found "markets," but they were still able to procure what they needed, not through kinfolk but as a result of the political economic arrangements that framed their studies. They held power and knew through power. These relations of power have occasionally been challenged in recent years, but in the main, little has changed. Anthropologists generally come to the "field" backed and funded by powerful institutions, and it is by virtue of the hierarchy they both represent and reproduce that they are able to produce knowledge. Increasingly, the distance between the knower and known is perceived and expressed in relation to money – access to credit and consumption practices are two obvious examples.

One of the challenges in contemporary anthropology is to differentiate between (a) money as a *concept* elaborated by philosophers and economists and (b) money as a *symbol* that participates in specific processes. Money, as a category in social science, has largely been elaborated from a

European perspective and defined by European historical experience – particularly the consolidation of nation-states, the expansion of capital and the rise of cities. Yet if European thought has been "indispensable" in understanding money as a subject of inquiry, it has also been "inadequate" (Chakrabarty 2000: 6) for describing the cultural practices that animate money in different societies.

Two of the key philosophers of money, Karl Marx and Georg Simmel, have provided important concepts related to money, including commoditization, alienation and individuation. Karl Marx theorizes the origins of money in barter (1977: 125–244; see Hart 2005, Maurer 2006, and Strathern 1992 for critiques). The money-form for Marx is a particular commodity that has been accepted by society as the "universal equivalent" (180). It is this social function, rather than any sensuous quality, that sets a particular commodity apart as "money." Georg Simmel (1990 [1907]) examines the parallel development of modern individualism and the expansion of the money economy. Money, he argues, comes to stand symbolically for the person, and thus functions as a kind of visible representation of an invisible interior. At the same time, he shows how money facilitates the keeping of secrets; money is small, easily carried and easily exchanged. It allows new forms of relationships to come into existence and flourish. Money, Simmel argued, circulates as the collective representation of society, a form of economic interdependence characteristic of industrial societies. Simmel's insights have been supported and developed by subsequent theorists of modernity (Giddens 1991, Harvey 1985) who have also characterized money as a quintessential instrument of modernity.

Anthropologists mindful of the epistemological problems of translating European concepts have drawn on European thinkers critical of markets and their expansion. In the first half of the twentieth century, Marcel Mauss (1967) and Karl Polanyi (1944) wrote seminal monographs on non-market exchanges, such as gift exchange. For Mauss, the gift was a "total social fact," an "underlying institution" that integrated various domains of social life including religion, kinship and politics through the entailed obligation of reciprocity. To give a gift, in other words, requires a return, and those relationships of reciprocity and asymmetry, argued Mauss, are central to human culture. Polanyi moved beyond gift exchange to examine the "market," which he viewed as an historical institution, created and maintained by nation-states. These two works have focused anthropological attention on the importance of reciprocal and redistributive transactional modes, which are generally seen as producing "social persons" (Weiner 1992). Moreover, these insights have provided a powerful counterweight to prevailing conceptions of the individual and private property of commercial societies (Strathern 1988).

Some of the early anthropological insights emerged from two simple questions: What counts as money, and How is money is counted? Anthropologists have used the descriptor "primitive" to distinguish "their" money from "our" money (Einzig 1949, Dalton 1965). Primitive money has been defined in contrast to modern money in two significant ways. First, it has been characterized by the lack of deliberate control by a political authority (e.g. national bank). Second, primitive money has been seen as not entirely impersonal, its circulation encoding dimensions of personhood such as age, rank or status. Some anthropologists, following Polanyi, argued that money circulates as the "surface expression" or manifestation of different social and economic organizations (Dalton 1965: 61). In societies where money has been the dominant medium for settling debts, paying taxes and even offering gifts, the transactional modes of reciprocity and redistribution have been defined by and against the "marketplace."

Anthropologists have found insights into money under conditions in which money transgresses culturally constructed boundaries. The paradigmatic ethnographic example is Paul Bohannan's (1955, 1959) discussion of "spheres of exchange." Bohannan describes three distinct spheres of exchange – subsistence goods, ceremonial objects and rights over women – that organized the social life of the Tiv, a group of people in West Africa. As young men engaged in long-distance trade, they accumulated colonial currency, and then converted it into socially valued goods, transforming traditional values expressed in kinship and other social relations. The practice of sister-exchange, for example, was replaced by bridewealth, a process documented elsewhere.

While state-issued currencies have been catalysts of disintegration, they have also been central to modern forms of social integration. By the mid-twentieth century, the paradigmatic money-form was territorial currency issued by a political state. Territorial currencies emerged out of political projects of consolidation including taxation and the establishments of national banks. In the Americas, bankers competed with central banks over the right to create currency (Helleiner 2003). Even in the United States, the "greenback" or U.S. dollar was not standardized until the 1930s (Zelizer 1999). Money also came to serve other state interests: paper money, to take one case, provided a vehicle for circulating pedagogical images supportive of the nation-state (Hewitt 1994, Hewitt 1995), and also served as a screen onto which people projected their desires and anxieties (Lemon 1998, Notar 2004, Truitt 2006).

More recently, anthropologists have documented political arguments over currency and its representational content, and they have examined the ways such debates relate to community formation (Hart 2005, Malaby 2002, Peebles 2002, Notar 2004). Currency reforms, such as the introduction of the Euro, have been of interest to anthropologists for some time (see Hart 2002, Peebles 2002). Borneman (1992: 147), for example, examines the role of the postwar currency reform in the construction of West Berlin narratives of identification (see also Friedrich [ed.] 1988). Also in this tradition, J.A. Dickinson's essay (this volume) examines the ways in which currency, visibility and secrecy play out in post-Soviet Ukraine. She finds that citizens view currency as a sign of political and administrative competence; if something seems wrong with money, it is because the politicians are incompetent.

One of the fundamental insights of anthropology has been that money is not a "disembedding mechanism" but a symbol summoned by specific practices and made meaningful within specific worldviews (see Bloch and Parry 1989: 19). Anthropologists have thus tended to emphasize the long-term reproduction of social relations and distinctive cultural constructions of reality. Some anthropologists have addressed the ways individuals represent money in moments of social upheaval and rapid economic transformation. The paradigmatic ethnographic example is Michael Taussig's (1980) description of workers in Bolivia and Columbia who symbolize the alienating qualities of capitalism through offerings to *El Tio* and baptisms of money. In the ritual of baptism, a coin is secretly substituted for a young child, thus endowing the coin with the magical power to reproduce itself. In other places, the foreignness of money as impersonal and indeterminate value-sign is represented as "dirty," "polluting," "hot" and "bitter" (Gamburd 2004, Walsh 2003, Comaroff and Comaroff 1999). The sudden influx of money often overturns hierarchies expressed in terms of age or rank as individuals convert windfalls of cash into prestige goods and status-based consumption (Walsh 2003).

If cash is difficult to assimilate into social relations, it is in part because people resist using money as a gift, particularly in commercial societies. Money is generally seen as "less soulful" than other commodities, less expressive of intimate relationships and knowledge, less firmly rooted in social realms outside the market. When money does serve as a gift, it struggles to convey the particularity of the giver and the recipient. Mere quantification inhibits money's conversion into a gift (see Zelizer 1994, Carrier 1997). In Japan and the United States, individuals conceal money by wrapping it, an act that simultaneously obscures the monetary content of the gift even as it emphasizes the non-monetary investment of the giver (Zelizer 1994, Rupp 2003). Similarly, during the Depression in the United States, gift-wrapping became a popular means of hiding poverty while signifying the specificity and depth of gift-exchange. Some anthropologists have described how the "quality of quantity" may be suppressed in certain arenas, such as when ritual specialists receive "gifts" from their clients, a point addressed by Holbraad (2005, see also Butler 2006, Kiernan 1988).

How then do people attempt to "personalize" money? Social research on money has demonstrated that while money may be "general purpose" (in contrast to "special purpose"), people nevertheless classify exchanges and the material with which they make them. This claim may seem intuitively obvious, in that it shows that people classify money just as they do other materials and concepts (see Kopytoff), but it reminds researchers to attend to the categories themselves; how, for example, do people distinguish among "gifts," "investment," "mad money," "allowance" or "spending money"? The meaning of money is also important in terms of the production and definition of personhood, particularly gender. Viviana Zelizer (1994) demonstrates how gendered practices including "pin money" and social insurance are important means by which individuals distinguish categories and types of money. In Southeast Asia, to take one example, women are often portrayed as having control over money, but their power cannot be equated with status, as Suzanne Brenner (1997) argues in her study of female traders in Java, Indonesia.

In China, the importance of exchange to relatedness is evident in the literature on *guanxi* (Smart 1993, Yang 1994, Pieke 1995). Yet when such exchanges include money, they put the logic of relatedness at risk. In religious practices, people use the social power of money to communicate with gods and ancestral spirits (Gates 1987), which are then ritually reproduced as the source of wealth. In some cases, people then attempt to re-appropriate that power by "borrowing" money from the temple spirits (Weller 2000). In this light, we can see why in China people relegate U.S. dollars to the sphere of gifts, while the Chinese *reminbi* circulates in the marketplace (Chu this volume, see Notar 2006 for an analysis of the anxieties around counterfeits). Ironically, it is the very pull of the U.S. dollar that contributes to the steady streams of labor and capital restructuring Chinese society.

Studies of post-socialist societies have provided compelling evidence of the tensions between state-market relations expressed through competing currency regimes. With the collapse of the Soviet Union, the demonetization of Soviet currency and the proliferation of national currencies, anthropologists have learned that money not only dissolves social ties, it can also lead to the formation of new communities. In these societies, global currencies have displaced state-issued currencies, life savings have been wiped out by inflation, black markets have competed robustly with state-owned channels of distribution, and the vast majority of people have struggled to get by on a day-to-day basis. Katherine Verdery (1995) examines the popularity of a pyramid-type scheme in Romania through which people began to distinguish between "my" money earned through labor and profit that accrued from their investment; the distinctions "enabled them to manipulate in their minds sums they had never imagined, to think about what they might do with such sums – to plan their expenditures – and to grow accustomed to thinking about larger and larger sums in a gradual way" (1995: 643). Other anthropologists have documented how, in the face of cash scarcity, people have substituted other commodities or currencies as money (Pine 2002, Reis 2002, Rogers 2005, Woodruff 1999a). J.A. Dickinson (this volume) examines the ways in which currency, visibility and secrecy play out in post-Soviet Ukraine.

The communities created by money are often structured around new relations of indebtedness. As the global U.S. dollar, the euro and locally issued currencies compete with territorial currencies, power becomes increasingly embodied in experts – economists, development specialists and financial experts (see Harper 1998 for analysis of the IMF). Competing currencies are a surface expression of a new world order, measuring not only market-value, but also the credibility of their issuing authorities (Lemon 1998, Malaby 2002, Maurer 2005, Dickinson this volume). Transformations of the global political economy and the declining capacity of State governments to influence market forces have shaped anthropological agendas (Coronil and Skurski 1991, Znoj 1998). The term "underdevelopment," for example, arose from the Bretton-Woods era of national political controls over domestic markets. Yet these controls were premised on a geographic ranking of the world that constructed the "Third World" as site of intervention for the excess capital of the "First World" (Escobar 1994). The collapse of the Bretton-Woods consensus initiated a period of disorganized capitalism, or what Gregory (1997) has called "savage money." Money is especially "savage" in countries dependent on global commodity markets where slight fluctuations in price can have enormous social costs.

Anthropologists have revised the very concept of culture in the face of the global interconnectedness engendered by commodity markets (see Tsing 2000). Studies of economic regulation, including those promoted by multinational organizations such as the International Monetary Fund (Roitman 2004, Ferguson 2006) have raised critical questions regarding control and sovereignty. Other anthropologists have turned to new ethnographic objects, including financial institutions and technocratic experts such as bankers or financial traders. These studies have focused on the role of networks, technologies of calculation, narratives and models of knowledge (Ho 2005, Riles 2004, Zaloom 2003, Harper 1998).

In addition to these studies, anthropologists have analyzed capital flows and commodity chains, and how these linkages are potentially creative sources of identification (see Bestor 2004, Mintz 1985). Shopping, for example, has long been recognized as an important domain through which people express their identity by consumption (Bourdieu 1984, Miller 1998, Veblen 1925). These studies highlight that the source of identification with money is not just in its accumulation or investment in profit-making enterprises, but also in its sheer expenditure, the delight in money's power of conversion into what it is not (Simmel 1990). At the same time, anthropologists have documented the popularity of American-style marketing approaches and self-management techniques for residents in cities like Bangkok or fraudulent schemes where people claim sources of identification not bound by kin obligations or patron-client relations (Wilson 2004, Smith 2001). Likewise, religious movements centered on prosperity, especially evangelicalism, provide a compelling framework for revaluing wealth in impoverished areas. In these movements, money becomes a symbol of the "holy spirit" (see Wiegele 2004 for an analysis of the El Shaddhai movement in the Philippines).

Money is a source of creativity in other contexts as well. Migration patterns organized around labor markets have been accompanied by transformations in gender and kin relations. Social research has focused on female labor in industrial factories, in part because women's access to wage-based labor has often diminished sources of male authority (Ong 1987, Salaff 1995, Wolf 1992). If migration is about the movement of people, it is also about the movement of money in the form of remittances, the conversion of wages earned in one place into gifts sent to another. It is through the transmission of money that many migrants maintain their social connections and, by extension, sources of identification (Cliggett 2003). The vast amount of money that is remitted to other places suggests new ways in which capitalism provides an infrastructure of sociality (Cohen 2001, Pedersen 2002, Osella and Osella 2000).

The essays in this volume contribute to the anthropological literature of what money means and what money does with a focus on ethnographers' own participation in the very processes they document. In so doing, they overturn some of the conventional understandings of money. It may seem that the essays replicate the conventions of ethnographic inquiry – face-to-face interactions that are conducted in non-Western contexts. Yet we hope this Guide to Further Reading alerts the reader to how these encounters are not bound by local conventions. Rather, it is money that summons complex grids of exchange. Transnational migration, overseas remittances, changing political regimes and transnational corporations are invoked in what otherwise seem to be simple transactions with money. In Pakistan, Naeem Inayatullah is received by kinfolk and friends as a beneficiary of the inequalities inherent in international labor markets. In Ghana and Germany, Senders experiences both plentitude and scarcity; yet in both fields, this relation to money generates insight and opportunity that cannot be purchased. He contrasts the analytical potential of anthropology against the conventional view of money's power, the American woman's complaint that "you can't get *anything*" in Ghana against the Aussiedler fantasy of America as a world of *"everything."*

If money is a medium for global interconnectedness, then those connections are hardly uniform. It should not be a surprise that the U.S. dollar emerges as a trope of globalizing relations. But it would be a mistake to attribute that power to the U.S. dollar alone. Julie Chu suggests that the ritualized haggling over prices in China marks the limits of the U.S. dollar's purchasing power. For J.A. Dickinson, the black-market premium for U.S. dollars vanishes as transactions for foreign-made commodities become increasingly commonplace. Ellen Moodie and Allison Truitt are nodes in the flow of U.S. dollars to El Salvador and Vietnam. In Moodie's hands, money appears to offer redemption for suffering, but for Truitt, money escapes social control, taking on its own life through unexpected forms of credit and indebtedness.

We hope that the reader has come to see money neither as a universally coherent concept nor as a culturally bound symbol, but as a rich source for anthropological analysis. It is only one of the mediums by which anthropologists reflect on the ethics of fieldwork and responsibility to others. This dilemma is expressed most forcefully by Marty Otanez's realization that his personal ethics are framed by ever-increasing geopolitical disparities in wealth. Moreover, he must also acknowledge that his key guide, a labor union leader, does not hold the same views towards Philip Morris as he does. In a different context, Senders finds himself implicated in relations of violence and power he cannot overtly support, but that he cannot control. Money, by facilitating new psychological identifications and new objects of desire, finally plays a powerful role in creating what anthropologists see as "culture."

Bibliography

Akin, D. and Robbins, J. (1999), *Money and Modernity: State and Local Currencies in Melanesia*, Pittsburgh: University of Pittsburgh Press.

Argueta, M. (1985), *One Day of Life*, translated by B. Brow, New York: Vintage International/Random House.

Bakhtin, M. (1983), "Discourse in the Novel," in M. Holoquist (ed. and trans), *The Dialogic Imagination: Four Essays*, Austin: University of Texas Press.

Behar, R. (1993), *Translated Woman: Crossing the Border with Esperanza's Story*, Boston: Beacon Press.

Behar, R. (1995), "Writing in my Father's Name: A Diary of Translated Woman's First Year," in R. Behar and D. Gordon (eds.), *Women Writing Culture*, Berkeley: University of California Press.

Behar, R. (1996), "Rage and Redemption: Reading the Life Story of a Mexican Marketing Woman," in D. Tedlock and B. Mannheim (eds.), *The Dialogic Emergence of Culture*, Urbana: University of Illinois Press.

Belk, R.W. and Wallendorf, M. (1990), "The Sacred Meanings of Money," *Journal of Economic Psychology*, 11: 35–67.

Berdahl, D. (1999), *Where the World Ended: Re-Unification and Identity in the German Borderland*, Berkeley: University of California Press.

Bestor, T.C. (2004), *Tsukiji: The Fish Market at the Center of the World*, Berkeley: University of California Press.

Bloch, M. and Parry, J. (1982), *Death and the Regeneration of Life*, Cambridge: Cambridge University Press.

Bloch, M. and Parry, J. (1989), "Introduction: Money and the Morality of Exchange," in J. Parry and M. Bloch (eds.), *Money and the Morality of Exchange*, Cambridge: Cambridge University Press.

Bohannan, P. (1955), "Some Principles of Exchange and Investment among the Tiv of Central Nigeria," *American Anthropologist*, 57: 60–70.

Bohannan, P. (1959), "The Impact of Money on an African Subsistence Economy," *Journal of Economic History*, 19: 491–503.

Borneman, J. (1992), *Belonging in the Two Berlins: Kin, State, Nation*, Cambridge: Cambridge University Press.

Bourdieu, P. (1984), *Distinction: A Social Critique of the Judgement of Taste*, translated by R. Nice, Cambridge, MA: Harvard University Press.

Brenner, S. (1997), *The Domestication of Desire*, Princeton, NJ: Princeton University Press.

Breton, S. (1999), "Social Body and Icon of the Person: A Symbolic Analysis of Shell Money Among the Wodani, Western Highlands of Irian Jaya," *American Ethnologist*, 26(3): 558–82.

Buchanan J. (1997), *Frozen Desire: The Meaning of Money*, New York: Farrar Straus Giroux.

Butler, N. (2006), "Costs of Knowledge: some Economic Underpinnings of Spiritual Relations in Islam in Niger," in N. Dannhaeuser and C. Werner (eds.), *Markets and Market Liberationalization: Ethnographic Reflections*, Oxford: Elsevier.

Caldwell, M. (2002), "The Taste of Nationalism: Food Politics in Postsocialist Moscow," *Ethnos*, 67(3): 295–319.

Carrier, J. (1997), *Meanings of the Market*, Oxford: Berg.

Chakrabarty, D. (2000), *Provincializing Europe: Postcolonial Thought and Historical Difference*, Princeton, NJ: Princeton University Press.

Cliggett, L. (2003), "Gift Remitting and Alliance Building in Zambian Modernity: Old Answers to Modern Problems," *American Anthropologist*, 105(3): 543–52.

Cohen, J. (2001), "Transnational Migration in Rural Oaxaca, Mexico: Dependency, Development, and the Household," *American Anthropologist*, 103(4): 954–67.

Comaroff, J. and Comaroff, J. (1999), "Occult Economies and the Violence of Abstraction: Notes from the South African Postcolony," *American Ethnologist*, 26(2): 279–303.

Cook, S. (1966), "The Obsolete Anti-market Mentality: A Critique of the Substantive Approach to Economic Anthropology," *American Anthropologist*, 68: 323–45.

Coronil, F. and J. Skurski (1991), "Dismembering and Remembering the Nation: The Semantics of Political Violence in Venezuela," *Comparative Studies of Society and History*, 33(2): 288–337.

Crump, T. (1981), *The Phenomenon of Money*, London: Routledge.

Dalton, G. (1965), "Primitive Money," *American Anthropologist*, 61(1): 44–65.

Dominguez, V. (1990), "Representing Value and the Value of Representation: A Different Look at Money," *Cultural Anthropologist*, 5(1): 16–44.

Douglas, M. (1958), "Raffia Cloth Distribution in the Lele Economy," *Africa*, 29: 109–22.

Einzig, P. (1949), *Primitive Money in its Ethnological, Historical, and Economic Aspects*, London: Eyre and Spottiswoode.

Eiss, P. (2002), "Hunting for the Virgin: Meat, Money, and Memory in Tetiz, Yucatan," *Cultural Anthropology*, 17(3): 291–330.

Elyachar, J. (2002), "Empowerment Money: The World Bank, Nongovernmental Organizations, and the Value of Culture in Egypt," *Public Culture*, 14(3): 493–513.

Escobar, A. (1994), *Encountering Development: The Making and Unmaking of the Third World*, Princeton, NJ: Princeton University Press.

Evans-Pritchard, E.E. (1940), *The Nuer: A Description of the Modes of Livelihood and Political Institutions of a Nilotic People*, Oxford: Oxford University Press.

Fabian, J. (1983), *Time and the Other: How Anthropology Makes its Object*, New York: Columbia University Press.

Ferguson, J. (2006), *Global Shadows: Africa in the Neoliberal World Order*, Durham, NC: Duke University Press.

Fforde, A. and de Vylder, S. (1996), *From Plan to Market: The Economic Transition in Vietnam*, Boulder, CO: Westview Press.

Foster, R. (1999), "In God We Trust? The Legitimacy of Melanesian Currencies," in D. Akin and J. Robbins (eds.), *Money and Modernity: State and Local Currencies in Melanesia*, Pittsburgh: University of Pittsburgh Press.

Frazer, J.G. (1922), *The Golden Bough: A Study in Magic and Religion*, New York: Macmillan.

Friedrich, H. (1988), *Mein Kopfgeld. Die Währungsreform – Rückblicke nach vier Jahrzehnten*, Munich: Deutscher Taschenbuch Verlag.

Gamburd, M.R. (2004), "Money that Burns Like Oil: A Sri Lankan Cultural Logic of Morality and Agency," *Ethnology*, 43(2): 167–84.

Gates, H. (1987), "Money for the Gods," *Modern China*, 13(3): 259–77.

Geschiere, P. (2000), "Money Versus Kinship: Subversion or Consolidation?" *The Asia Pacific Journal of Anthropology*, 1(1): 54–78.

Giddens, A. (1991), *Consequences of Modernity*, Stanford, CA: Stanford University Press.

Gilbert, E. (2005), "Common Cents: Situating Money in Time and Place," *Economic Sociology*, 34(3): 357–88.

Gregory, C.A. (1997), *Savage Money: The Anthropology and Politics of Commodity Exchange*, Amsterdam: Harwood Academic.

Guyer, J. (1994a), *Money Matters: Instability, Values and Social Payments in the Modern History of West African Communities*, Portsmouth, NH: Heinemann.

Guyer, J. (1994b), "Introduction: The Currency Interface and its Dynamics," in J. Guyer (ed.), *Money Matters: Instability, Values and Social Payments in the Modern History of West African Communities*, Portsmouth, NH: Heinemann.

Habermas, J. (1991), *The Structural Transformation of the Public Sphere: An Inquiry into a Category of Bourgeois Society*, Cambridge, MA: MIT Press.

Harper, R.P. (1998), *Inside the IMF: An Ethnography of Documents, Technology and Organisational Action*, San Diego: Academic Press.

Hart, K. (1986), "Heads or Tails? Two Sides of the Coin," *Man*, 21: 637–56.

Hart, K. (2001), *The Memory Bank: Money in an Unequal World*, New York and London: Texere.

Hart, K. (2002), "Comment – The Euro," *Anthropology Today*, 18(1): 20.

Hart, K. (2005), "Notes Towards an Anthropology of Money," *Kritikos*, 2.

Harvey, D. (1985), *Consciousness and the Urban Experience*, Baltimore, MD: Johns Hopkins University Press.

Helleiner, E. (2003), *The Making of National Money: Territorial Currencies in Historical Perspective*, Ithaca, NY: Cornell University Press.

Hewitt, V. (1994), *Beauty and the Banknote: Images of Women on Paper Money*, London: British Museum.

Hewitt, V. (1995), *The Banker's Art: Studies in Paper Money*, London: British Museum.

Ho, K. (2005), "Situating Global Capitalisms: A View from Wall Street Investment Banks," *Cultural Anthropology*, 20(1): 68–96.

Holbraad, M. (2005), "Expending Multiplicity: Money in Cuban Ifa Cults," *Journal of the Royal Anthropological Institute*, 11: 231–254.

Humphrey, C. (2002), *The Unmaking of Soviet Life: Everyday Economies after Socialism*, Ithaca, NY: Cornell University Press.

Hutchinson, S. (1996), *Nuer Dilemmas: Coping with Money, War and the State*, Berkeley: University of California Press.

Keane, W. (2001), "Money is No Object: Materiality, Desire and Modernity in an Indonesian Society," in F. Myers (ed.), *The Empire of Things*, Santa Fe: SAR Press.

Kiernan, J.P. (1988), "The Other Side of the Coin: The Conversion of Money to Religious Purposes in Zulu Zionist Churches," *Man*, 23: 453–68.

Kopytoff, I. (1986), "The Cultural Biography of Things: Commoditization as Process," in A. Appadurai (ed.), *The Social Life of Things: Commodities in Cultural Perspective*, Cambridge: Cambridge University Press.

Lambek, M. (2001), "The Value of Coins in a Sakalava Polity: Money, Death, and Historicity in a Mahajanga, Madagascar," *Comparative Studies in Society and History*, 43: 735–62

Lemon, A. (1998), "Your Eyes are Green like Dollars: Counterfeit Cash, National Substance, and Currency Apartheid in 1990s Russia," *Cultural Anthropology*, 13(1): 22–55.

Levine, D. (1977), *Economic Studies: Contributions to the Critique of Political Economy*, New York: Routledge Kegan and Paul.

Levine, D. (1978), *Economic Theory: The Elementary Relations of Economic Life, Volume I*, New York: Routledge Kegan and Paul.

Luong, H.V. (2003), "Introduction: Postwar Vietnamese Society: An Overiew of Transformational Dynamics," in H.V. Luong (ed.), *Postwar Vietnam: Dynamics of a Transforming Society*, Lanham, MD: Rowman and Littlefield.

Malaby, T.M. (2002), "Making Change in the New Europe: Euro Competence in Greece," *Anthropological Quarterly*, 75(3): 591–97.

Marcus, G. (1999), "The Uses of Complicity and the Changing Mise-en-Scene of Anthropological Fieldwork," in S. Ortner (ed.), *The Fate of "Culture": Geertz and Beyond*, Berkeley: University of California Press.

Marx, K. (1977), *Capital: A Critique of Political Economy*, New York: Vintage Books.

Maurer, B. (2005), *Mutual Life, Ltd: Islamic Banking, Alternative Currencies, Lateral Reason*, Princeton, NJ: Princeton University Press.

Maurer, B. (2006), "The Anthropology of Money," *Annual Reviews of Anthropology*, 35: 15-36.

Mauss, M. (1967), *The Gift*, New York: Beacon Press.

Miller, D. (1998), *A Theory of Shopping, Ithaca*, NY: Cornell University Press.

Mintz, S. (1985), *Sweetness and Power: the Place of Sugar in Modern History*, New York: Penguin Books.

Moodie, E. (2002), *It's Worse than War: Telling Everyday Danger in Postwar San Salvador*, Ph.D. dissertation, Ann Arbor: University of Michigan.

Nader, L. (1974), "Up the Anthropologist – Perspectives Gained from Studying Up," in D. Hymes (ed.), *Reinventing Anthropology*, New York: Pantheon Books.

Nelson, D. (1999), *A Finger in the Wound: Body Politics in Quincentennial Guatemala*, Berkeley: University of California Press.

Notar, B. (2004), "Ties that Dissolve and Bind: Competing Currencies, Prestige, and Politics in Early Twentieth-Century China," in C. Werner and D. Bell, *Values and Valuables: From the Sacred to the Symbolic*, Walnut Creek, CA: AltaMira Press.

Notar, B. (2006), "Authenticity, Anxiety and Counterfeit Confidence: Outsourcing Souvenirs, Changing Money, and Narrating Value in Reform-Era China," *Modern China*, 32(1): 64–98.

Ong, A. (1987), *Spirits of Resistance and Capitalist Discipline: Factory Women in Malaysia*, Albany, NY: State University of New York Press.

Osella, F. and Osella, C. (2000), "Migration, Money and Masculinity in Kerala," *The Journal of the Royal Anthropological Institute*, 6(1): 117–33.

Pedersen, D. (2002), "The Storm We Call Dollars: Determining Value and Belief in El Salvador and the United States," *Cultural Anthropology*, 17(3): 431–59.

Peebles, G. (2002), "Comment – The Euro," *Anthropology Today*, 18(1): 20.

Peebles, G. (2004), "The Crown Capitulates: National Currency and Global Capital in the Swedish Currency Crisis," in C. Garsten and M. De Montoya, *Market Matters: Exploring Cultural Processes in the Global Marketplace*, New York: Palgrave MacMillan.

Pieke, F.N. (1995), "Bureaucracy, Friends, and Money: The Growth of Capital Socialism in China," *Comparative Studies in Society and History*, 37(3): 494–518.

Pine, F. (2002), "Dealing with Money: Złotys, Dollars and Other Currencies in the Polish Highlands," in R. Mandel and C. Humphrey (eds.), *Markets and Moralities: Ethnographies of Post-Socialism*, Oxford: Berg.

Plattner, S. (1989), "Introduction," in S. Plattner (ed.), *Economic Anthropology*, Stanford, CA: Stanford University Press.

Polanyi, K. (1944), *The Great Transformation*, Boston: Beacon.

Rabinow, P. (1986), "Representations are Social Facts: Modernity and Post-Modernity in Anthropology," in J. Clifford and G.E. Marcus (eds.), *Writing Culture: The Poetics and Politics of Writing Ethnography*, Berkeley: University of California Press.

Rausing, S. (2004), *History, Memory, and Identity in Post-Soviet Estonia: The End of a Collective Farm*, Oxford: Oxford University Press.

Reis, N. (2002), "'Honest Bandits' and 'Warped People': Russian Narratives about Money, Corruption, and Moral Decay," in C. Greenhouse, E. Mertz and K. Warren (eds.), *Ethnography in Unstable Places*, Durham, NC: Duke University Press.

Riles, A. (2004), "Real Time: Unwinding Technocratic and Anthropological Knowledge," *American Ethnologist*, 31(3): 392–405.

Robbins, J. and Akin. D. (1999), "An Introduction to Melanesian Currencies: Agency, Identity, and Social Reproduction," in D. Akin and J. Robbins (eds.), *Money and Modernity: State and Local Currencies in Melanesia*, Pittsburgh: University of Pittsburgh Press.

Rogers, D. (2005), "Moonshine, Money, and the Politics of Liquidity in Rural Russia," *American Ethnologist*, 32(1): 63–81.

Roitman, J. (2004), *Fiscal Disobedience: An Anthropology of Economic Regulation in Central Africa*, Princeton, NJ: Princeton University Press.

Rupp, K. (2003), *Gift-giving in Japan: Cash, Connections, and Cosmologies*, Stanford, CA: Stanford University Press.

Rutherford, D. (2001), "Intimacy and Alienation: Money and the Foreign in Biak," *Public Culture*, 13(2): 63–81.

Salaff, J.W. (1995), *Working Daughters of Hong Kong: Filial Piety or Power in the Family?* New York: Columbia University Press.

Saul, M. (2004), "Money in Colonial Transition: Cowries and Francs in West Africa," *American Anthropologist*, 106(1): 71–84.

Senders, S. (2004) "What Do You Want Me to Do, Bang My Head Against the Wall?: Reflections on Having and Not Having in the Field." Presented as part of the panel, "Encounters with Money in the Field," Annual Meeting of the American Ethnological Society, April 22–5 in Atlanta, GA.

Simmel, G. (1950), "The Secret and the Secret Society," in K.H. Woff, (ed. and trans.), *The Sociology of Georg Simmel*, New York: Free Press.

Simmel, G. (1990 [1907]), *The Philosophy of Money*, London: Routledge.

Smart, A. (1993). "Gifts, Bribes, and Guanxi. A Reconsideration of Bourdieu's Social Capital," *Cultural Anthropology*, 8(3): 388–408.

Smith, D. (2001), "Ritual Killing, 419, and Fast Wealth: Inequality and the Popular Imagination in Southeastern Nigeria", *American Ethnologist*, 28(4): 803–26.

Stoller, P. (2002), *Money has No Smell: The Africanization of New York City*, Chicago: University of Chicago Press.

Strathern, M. (1988), *Gender of the Gift: Problems with Women and Problems with Society in Melanesia*, Berkeley: University of California Press.

Strathern, M. (1992), "Qualified Value: the Perspective of Gift Exchange," in C. Humphrey and S. Hugh-Jones (eds.), *Barter, Exchange and Value: An Anthropological Approach*, Cambridge: Cambridge University Press.

Taussig, M. (1980), *The Devil and Commodity Fetishism in South America*, Chapel Hill: University of North Carolina Press.

Truitt, A. (2006), "Big Money, New Money, and ATMs: Valuing Vietnamese Currency in Ho Chi Minh City," in N. Dannhaueser and Cynthia Werner (eds.), *Markets and Market: Liberalization: Ethnographic Reflections*, Oxford: Elsevier.

Tsing, A. (2000), "Inside the Economy of Appearances," *Public Culture*, 12(1): 115–44.

Veblen, T. (1925), *Theory of the Leisure Class: An Economic Study of Institutions*, London: George Allen and Unwin.

Verdery, K. (1995), "Faith, Hope and Caritas in the Land of the Pyramids, Romania, 1990 to 1994," *Comparative Studies in Society and History*, 37(4): 625–69.

Verdery, K. (1996), *What was Socialism, and What Comes Next?* Princeton, NJ: Princeton University Press.

Walsh, A. (2003), "'Hot Money' and Daring Consumption in a Northern Malagasy Sapphire-mining Town," *American Ethnologist*, 30(2): 290–305.

Weatherford, J. (1998), *The History of Money*, New York: Crown.

Weiner, A. (1992), *Inalienable Possessions: The Paradox of Keeping-while-Giving*, Berkeley: University of California Press.

Weller, R. (2000), "Living at the Edge: Religion, Capitalism, and the End of the Nation-State, *Public Culture*, 12(2): 477–98.

Wiegele, K. (2004), *Investing in Miracles: El Shaddai and the Transformation of Popular Catholicism in the Philippines*, Honolulu: University of Hawai'i Press.

Wilson, A. (2004), *Intimate Economies of Bangkok: Tomboys, Tycoons, and Avon Ladies in the Global City*, Berkeley: University of California Press.

Wolf, D. (1992), *Factory Daughters: Gender, Household Dynamics, and Rural Industrialization in Java*, Berkeley: University of California Press.

Woodruff, D. (1999a), "Barter of the Bankrupt: The Politics of Demonetization in Russia's Federal State," in M. Burawoy and K. Verdery (eds.), *Uncertain Transition: Ethnographies of Change in the Post-Socialist World*, New York: Rowman and Littlefield.

Woodruff, D. (1999b), *Money Unmade: Barter and the Fate of Russian Capitalism*, Ithaca, NY: Cornell University Press.

Yang, M (1994), *Gifts, Favors and Banquets: The Art of Social Relationships in China*, Ithaca, NY: Cornell University Press.

Zaloom, C. (2003), "Ambiguous Numbers: Trading Technologies and Interpretation in Financial Markets," *American Ethnologist*, 30(2): 258–72.

Zelizer, V. (1994), *Social Meanings of Money*, New York: Basic Books.

Zelizer, V. (1998), "How People talk about Money," *American Behavioral Scientist*, 41(10): 1373–83.

Zelizer, V. (1999), "Official Standardization vs. Social Differentiation in Americans' Uses of Money," in E. Gilbert and E. Helleiner (eds.), *Nation-states and Money: The Past, Present and Future of National Currencie 13 at the moments*, London: Routledge.

Znoj, H. (1998), "Hot Money and War Debts: Transactional Regimes in Southwestern Sumatra," *Comparative Study of Society and History*, 40: 193–222.

Index